UNCOVERING TRUMP

The Truth Behind Donald Trump's
Charitable Giving

David A. Fahrenthold

**Winner of the 2017 Pulitzer Prize
for National Reporting**

The Washington Post

DIVERSIONBOOKS

Diversion Books
A Division of Diversion Publishing Corp.
443 Park Avenue South, Suite 1008
New York, New York 10016
www.DiversionBooks.com

For more information, email info@diversionbooks.com

First Diversion Books edition April 2017.
Print ISBN: 978-1-63576-159-7
eBook ISBN: 978-1-63576-158-0

CONTENTS

The behind-the-scenes story of my year   1
    covering Trump

THE STORIES

What ever happened to all that money Trump raised   29
    for the veterans?

Missing from Trump's list of charitable giving: 37
    His own personal cash

Four months after fundraiser, Trump says he gave   52
    $1 million to veterans group

Trump promised millions to charity. We found less   58
    than $10,000 over 7 years.

Trump promised personal gifts on 'Celebrity   68
    Apprentice.' Here's who really paid.

Trump pays IRS a penalty for his foundation   78
    violating rules with gift to aid Florida
    attorney general

How Donald Trump retooled his charity to   86
    spend other people's money

Trump used $258,000 from his charity to   100
    settle legal problems

Trump Foundation ordered to stop fundrais-   112
    ing by N.Y. attorney general's office

Trump recorded having extremely lewd   119
    conversation about women in 2005

Trump boasts about his philanthropy. But his   127
    giving falls short of his words.

Donald Trump plans to shut down his char-   148
    itable foundation, which has been under
    scrutiny for months

Appendix   155

Photo illustration of David Fahrenthold by Bill O'Leary/The Washington Post

THE BEHIND-THE-SCENES STORY OF MY YEAR COVERING TRUMP

By David A. Fahrenthold
Dec. 27, 2016

"Arnold and Tim, if you'd come up, we're going to give you a nice, beautiful check," Donald Trump said. He held up an oversize check, the kind they give to people who win golf tournaments. It was for $100,000. In the top-left corner the check said: "The Donald J. Trump Foundation."

Along the bottom, it had the slogan of Trump's presidential campaign: "Make America Great Again."

This was in February.

The beginning of it.

Trump was in Waterloo, Iowa, for a caucus-day rally at the Five Sullivan Brothers Convention Center — named for five local siblings who had been assigned to the same

Navy cruiser in World War II. They all died when the ship went down at Guadalcanal.

Trump had stopped his rally to do something presidential candidates don't normally do. He was giving away money.

Arnold and Tim, whom he had called to the stage, were from a local veterans group. Although their big check had Trump's name on it, it wasn't actually Trump's money. Instead, the cash had been raised from other donors a few days earlier, at a televised fundraiser that Trump had held while he skipped a GOP debate because of a feud with Fox News.

Trump said he had raised $6 million that night, including a $1 million gift from his own pocket. Now Trump was giving it, a little at a time, to charities in the towns where he held campaign events.

"See you in the White House," one of the men said to Trump, leaving the stage with this check that married a nonprofit's name and a campaign's slogan.

"He said, 'We'll see you in the White House,' " Trump repeated to the crowd. "That's nice."

After that, Trump lost Iowa.

He won New Hampshire.

Then he stopped giving away money.

But as far as I could tell, just over $1.1 million had been given away. Far less than what Trump said he raised. And there was no sign of the $1 million Trump had promised from his own pocket.

So what happened to the rest of the money?

It sounded like an easy question that the Trump campaign could answer quickly. I thought I'd be through with the story in a day or two.

I was wrong.

That was the start of nine months of work for me, trying to dig up the truth about a part of Trump's life that he wanted to keep secret. I didn't understand — and I don't think Trump understood, either — where that one check, and that one question, would lead.

I'VE BEEN A REPORTER FOR THE WASHINGTON POST SINCE 2000, covering everything from homicide scenes in the District to Congress to the World Championship Muskrat Skinning Contest. (People race to see who skins a dead muskrat the fastest. There's also a beauty pageant. Some women compete in both.)

By the time I got to that Trump event in Waterloo, I'd been covering the 2016 presidential election for 13 months, since the last weeks of 2014. But I had the track record of a mummy's curse: Just about every campaign I had touched was dead.

I had, for instance, covered former New York governor George Pataki's (failed) attempt to get people to recognize him in a New Hampshire Chipotle. Pataki dropped out. I read the collected works of former Arkansas governor Mike Huckabee and made a list of everything the old Baptist preacher had ever condemned as immoral or untoward. The subjects of his condemnation ranged from college-age women going braless to dogs wearing clothes to Beyoncé. Huckabee condemned me. Then he dropped out, too.

I went to St. Louis to write about a speech given by former Texas governor Rick Perry. In the middle of the speech, Perry dropped out.

So by the time the New Hampshire primaries were over, the candidates I had covered were kaput. I needed a new beat. While I pondered what that would be, I decided to do a short story about the money Trump had raised for veterans.

I wanted to chase down two suspicions I'd brought home with me from that event in Iowa. For one thing, I thought Trump might have broken the law by improperly mixing his foundation with his presidential campaign. I started calling experts.

"I think it's pretty clear that that's over the line," Marc S. Owens, the former longtime head of the Internal Revenue Service's nonprofit division, told me when I called him.

Then Owens kept talking, and the story started deflating.

In theory, Owens said, nonprofit groups like the Trump Foundation are "absolutely prohibited" from participating or intervening in a political campaign. But, he said, if the IRS did investigate, it wouldn't likely start until the Trump Foundation filed its paperwork for 2016. Which wouldn't be until late 2017. Then an agent would open a case. There went 2018. Finally, Owens said, the IRS might take action: It might even take away the Trump Foundation's tax-exempt status.

In 2019. Or maybe not ever.

Owens doubted that the IRS — already under scrutiny from the GOP-run Congress after allegations it had given undue scrutiny to conservative groups — would ever pick a fight with Trump.

"I don't think anything's going to happen" to Trump, Owens said. "But, theoretically, it could."

My other suspicion was that Trump was still sitting on the bulk of the money he had raised for veterans — including the $1 million he had promised from himself.

I asked Trump's people to account for all this money. They didn't.

Then, finally, I got a call.

"The money is fully spent," Corey Lewandowski, then Trump's campaign manager, told me in late May. "Mr. Trump's money is fully spent."

But, Lewandowski told me, the details of Trump's $1 million in gifts were secret. He wouldn't say which groups Trump had donated to. Or when. Or in what amounts.

This was an important assertion — that Trump had delivered on a signature campaign promise — made without proof. I didn't want to just take Lewandowksi's word for it.

So I tried to prove him right.

I spent a day searching for Trump's money on Twitter, asking vets' organizations if they'd gotten any of it. I used Trump's Twitter handle, @realdonaldtrump, because I wanted Trump to see me searching.

Trump saw.

The next night, he called me to say he had just then given away the $1 million, all in one swoop, to a nonprofit run by a friend. That meant when Lewandowski said Trump's money was "fully spent," it was actually still in Trump's pocket.

On the phone, I asked Trump: Would you really have given this money away if I hadn't been asking about it?

"You know, you're a nasty guy," he said. "You're really a nasty guy."

A few days later, Trump held a news conference in Trump Tower, where he answered my other question. Where was the remainder of the money Trump had raised from other donors, four months earlier? Turns out, it had been sitting in the Trump Foundation, unspent. In this news conference, Trump announced that he had given the last of it away — and he lashed out at the media for asking him to account for the money.

"Instead of being like, 'Thank you very much, Mr. Trump,' or 'Trump did a good job,' everyone said : 'Who got it? Who got it? Who got it?' And you make me look very bad," Trump said. "I have never received such bad publicity for doing such a good job."

Because my stories had led to this angry moment, I was on "Morning Joe" and CNN and Lawrence O'Donnell. The New York Times and Le Monde referenced my work. My dad wrote to say how proud he was of me. I read pundits predicting that the presidential race itself would change. They said the old trope about Trump — that he was a Teflon candidate, immune to accountability — was now disproved.

When I came home from my last TV hit, the kids, ages 4 and 5 months, were asleep. The house was quiet. I was still full of caffeine and do-gooder energy and decided to tidy up.

Among the clutter on the coffee table, I found my 4-year-old's Party Popper, a bright yellow gun that fired confetti. For some reason, I held the gun up to my eye and looked down the barrel, the way Yosemite Sam always does.

It looked unloaded.

Then, for some reason, I pulled the trigger.

When I got to the ER, I had a swollen face, metal-foil confetti in my hair and a faint odor of gun smoke. Finally, the doctor could see me.

"I shot myself in the eye with a glitter gun," I said. I showed him the Party Popper, which I had brought with me, in case he wanted to send it off to the National Institute of Morons for further study.

I GOT HOME FROM THE HOSPITAL WITH A SCRATCHED cornea and a tube of eye ointment. The next day, with some of my dignity permanently lost, I got started on a bigger story.

The idea for this story had come from our executive editor, Marty Baron. One night, as we both waited for an elevator, Marty offered a suggestion.

Why don't you go beyond Trump's promises to give to veterans, he said, and look at Trump's giving to charity, period?

The logic was that Trump had just tried to wiggle out of a charitable promise he'd made on national TV. What, Marty wondered, had he been doing before the campaign, when nobody was looking?

That reporting process started with a lot of paper.

Working with one of The Post's ace researchers, Alice Crites, I went digging for records that would reveal Trump's charitable giving, going back to his early days as a Manhattan developer in the 1980s. We looked at old news clippings, detailing Trump's public statements. And we looked at tax filings from the Donald J. Trump Foundation, which had been dug out of storage by New York state.

Those two sources told two very different stories.

In the news clippings, you could see that Trump had repeatedly made public promises to donate to charity. In the 1980s, for instance, Trump had promised to give away $4 million from sales of his book "The Art of the Deal." In more recent years, he said he would give away $2.5 million he made off "The Apprentice." And donated the profits from Trump University. All told, the pledges in those news clips made it seem that Trump had given away more than $12 million.

In more recent clippings, in fact, Trump's presidential campaign staff said his actual giving had been far higher than that: "tens of millions " over his lifetime.

The state's records showed something else.

They showed that the Trump Foundation — which Trump had set up to give away his own money — had received only a total of $5.5 million from Trump since 1987.

So where was all that other money that he said he had been donating?

"We want to keep them private. We want to keep them quiet," Allen Weisselberg, the chief financial officer of Trump's business, had told me about the missing money. "He doesn't want other charities to see it. Then it becomes like a feeding frenzy."

Once again, I didn't want to take his word for it.

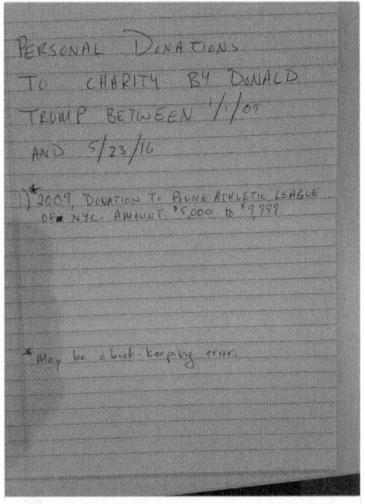

PERSONAL DONATIONS
TO CHARITY BY DONALD
TRUMP BETWEEN 1/1/09
AND 5/23/16

1) *2009, DONATION TO POLICE ATHLETIC LEAGUE
OF NYC. AMOUNT $5,000 to $9,999

* May be a book-keeping error.

David Fahrenthold ✓
@Fahrenthold

[▾ Follow]

Once again: if @realdonaldtrump gave your charity $, or gave
your child a @timtebow helmet, DM me. This is all I got

11:28 AM - 25 Jul 2016

↩ ⟲ 138 ♥ 180

So I set out — using Twitter — to try to prove Trump right.

I started making a list of charities I thought were most likely to have received money from Trump's own pocket. Nonprofits that had received donations from the Trump Foundation. Charities whose galas Trump had attended. Causes he'd praised on Twitter.

In each case, I called the charity and asked if it had ever received a donation from Trump — and, if so, when. Then, I wrote the charity's name and its response on a legal pad and posted pictures of the legal pad to Twitter.

My list started to grow: 100 charities. 150. 200.

In all those calls, a pattern began to emerge. In the years between 2008 and 2015 — when Trump wasn't giving money to the Trump Foundation — he didn't seem to have given much to other people's charities, either. The only gift I could find in that range was from 2009, when he was credited with giving less than $10,000 to the Police Athletic League of New York City.

250 charities.

As the circus of the 2016 campaign swirled around me — Twitter beefs, Trump's criticisms of a Gold Star family and a Mexican American federal judge — I stayed focused on this small slice of Trump's life. After a while, my 4-year-old daughter started talking about the Trump Foundation at dinner, just because her parents talked about nothing else. "He should give the money to the people, so the people get the money," she said. "It's not nice."

I called 300 charities.

325.

This story started to remind me of one of the weirdest

stories I've ever done: a 2014 tale about the federal government's giant paperwork cave.

The cave was about 45 minutes north of Pittsburgh. The Office of Personnel Management kept federal employees' personnel records in 28,000 file cabinets inside the caverns of an abandoned limestone mine. There were 600 federal employees down there. Cave clerks. Their job was to assemble and collate paperwork from the caverns and use that paperwork to compute how much individual federal employees would receive in benefits when they retired. The cave clerks worked in an absurdist parody of government inefficiency, which was as slow in 2014 as it was in the 1970s.

In reporting jargon, I'd tried the front door: I asked to tour the mine. OPM said no. So then I went looking for windows. I sought out ex-employees, who had firsthand knowledge of the place but weren't beholden to OPM's desire for secrecy.

I found them. By piecing together their recollections, I got the story that the government didn't want me to find.

Now Trump himself was the abandoned limestone mine.

If he wouldn't tell me what he had given away, I'd try to find the answer anyway — by talking to charities with firsthand knowledge of what he had given.

When I reached No. 325 on my list, I yanked on a window, and it gave.

"They ended up purchasing a Michael Israel portrait of Donald Trump," said Matthew Ladika, the CEO of a Florida children's charity called HomeSafe.

I had called this charity — which I knew had received $20,000 from the Trump Foundation — to ask if it had ever received anything else, from Trump's own pocket. It had not. But Ladika told me something I didn't expect: the reason for that $20,000 gift from Trump's charity.

Trump had used it to buy a portrait of himself.

The portrait had been painted by a "speed painter," who was the entertainment at a charity gala at Trump's Mar-a-Lago Club. Melania Trumpbought it for $20,000. But then, later, Trump paid for it with a check from the Trump Foundation.

That raised a new set of questions. Tax law prohibits "self-dealing," which is when charity leaders use their non-profits' money to buy things for themselves. If Trump hung that portrait on the wall at one of his resorts, for instance, he'd be breaking the law. So where was the portrait now?

I asked Trump's people. They didn't respond.

I tried a Google Images search, feeding it a photo of the portrait, which showed Trump's painted face.

"Best guess for this image: Orange," Google said.

I got a screen full of oranges. Orange juice. Orange Julius. No portraits.

I kept looking, posting details of my search to Twitter. Soon I had attracted a virtual army, ready to join the scavenger hunt. I had begun the year with 4,700 Twitter followers. By September I had more than 60,000 and climbing fast. I began hearing from celebrities and even a few personal heroes, offering their assistance out of the blue. The barbecue columnist for Texas Monthly — an idol to me, as a journalist and a native Texan — was watching videos of other people's parties taken at a Trump golf resort. He thought he'd spotted the painting in the background (he hadn't). Kathy Griffin, the actress, called me with her memories about visiting the set of Trump's "The Celebrity Apprentice." Mark Cuban, the Dallas Mavericks owner, was sending me links on Twitter, new leads on Trump promises.

That army — almost all of them strangers to me — never found the first portrait. But soon there was a new target and a new scavenger hunt.

"Google 'Havi Art Trump,' " said a strange voice on the phone one day, calling from the 561 area code. Palm Beach, Fla.

David Fahrenthold ✔
@Fahrenthold

🐦 Follow

ALSO...There is another. @realDonaldTrump bought 2nd portrait of himself w/ charity money. This time, for $10K.
washingtonpost.com/politics/trump...
10:34 AM - 20 Sep 2016

↩ 🔁 1,238 ♥ 1,088

I did.

The Google search revealed a new portrait of Trump. This one was four feet tall, painted by Miami artist Havi Schanz. After a phone call, I confirmed that Trump had purchased it in 2014 at a charity auction run by the Unicorn Children's Foundation. Once again, he had the Trump Foundation pay the bill.

I needed to find that portrait. I turned to my Twitter followers, putting out a photo of the new $10,000 portrait.

That was at 10:34 a.m.

By early evening I knew where it was.

"The Havi Painting was at Doral National in Miami, you can see two separate pics that tourists have taken of it," wrote Allison Aguilar.

I've never met Aguilar. I learned later that she is a former HR manager who is now a stay-at-home mother in Atlanta, writing short stories on the side. Days before, looking for the $20,000 portrait, she had scoured the website for Trump's golf resort at Doral, in Florida, scanning more than 500 user-generated photos of the resort's rooms, restaurants and golf course.

About halfway through, she had spotted another portrait in a photo, hanging on a wall at the resort.

Then she saw my tweet, saying that I was now looking for that portrait, too.

"Oh, now *that* I've seen," Aguilar remembered thinking.

The TripAdvisor photo she found was dated February 2016.

Was the portrait still there?

The answer was provided by another stranger.

Enrique Acevedo, an anchor at the Spanish-language

 Enrique Acevedo ✓
@Enrique_Acevedo

🐦 Follow

Hey @Fahrenthold just checked and the portrait is still hanging at the Champions Lounge. How much did you say it cost the Trump Foundation?

12:32 AM - 21 Sep 2016

↩ ⟲ 546 ♥ 771

network Univision, saw my tweet that night, broadcasting that Aguilar had traced the portrait to Doral. Acevedo realized that Doral was just a few blocks from the Univision studios. He booked a room for that night.

"I used points," Acevedo said. "I didn't want to ... spend any money on Trump's property, so I used points." After his newscast ended, Acevedo checked in and started quizzing the late-night cleaning crews.

"Have you seen this picture?" he asked. "They said, 'Oh yeah, it's downstairs.' "

Bingo. Acevedo found the $10,000 portrait, paid for with charity money, hanging on the wall of the resort's sports bar.

"Hey @Fahrenthold just checked and the portrait is still hanging at the Champions Lounge. How much did you say it cost the Trump Foundation?" he wrote on Twitter that night.

All of that — from my first request for help to Acevedo's discovery — had taken less than 14 hours. Together, we had discovered Trump doing exactly what the law said he couldn't do: using his charity's money to decorate his resort.

A Trump spokesman later offered the explanation that the resort was actually doing the foundation a favor, by storing its art free of charge. Tax experts were not impressed by this reasoning.

"It's hard to make an IRS auditor laugh," one told me. "But this would do it."

• • •

On a morning in October, a month before Election Day, a window opened itself.

I got a phone call. It was a source, with a video.

The first few seconds were jumpy footage of a bus, lumbering through a bland Hollywood backlot. The soundtrack was indistinct mumbling. But then there was Trump's voice.

"I moved on her, actually. You know, she was down in Palm Beach. I moved on her. And I failed. I'll admit it," he was saying. "I did try and f--- her. She was married."

That was 17 seconds in.

On the bus were Trump and "Access Hollywood" host Billy Bush. The video, I figured out, had been shot in 2005. The two men were visiting the set of NBC's "Days of Our Lives," where Trump was to make a cameo appearance. In a blaze of network synergy, NBC's "Access Hollywood" was there to see Trump arrive. Trump and Bush were wearing hot microphones.

On the bus, Trump told Bush about trying and failing to seduce a woman in Palm Beach. ("I took her out furniture shopping," he said.)

Trump also described how he kissed and groped women, without asking first.

"And when you're a star, they let you do it!" Trump said. The thing that stood out to me was the genuine wonder in his voice. He seemed to be saying: I can't believe it either, but the world lets you get away with this.

This was not the first time Trump had been recorded having lewd conversations. BuzzFeed, in particular, had found tapes of Trump talking about women with shock jock Howard Stern. ("You could've gotten her, right? You could've nailed her," Stern asked him once about Princess Diana, who at the time had recently died. "I think I could have," Trump said.) But those had been excused, by some, because they were just words. Trump, it seemed, was playing an outrageous version of himself in public, for the entertainment of Stern and his audience.

But this video was different. This was Trump talking, in private, about his own conduct: how, when and why he groped women. It was not a story about words. It was about Trump's actions, which these words revealed for the first time.

I first made myself into Paul Revere of the cubicles, raising alarms around the newsroom and setting people in motion. The Post's video team started to edit, transcribe and subtitle the footage. They told me they would be ready to post a version of the video at about 3:30 p.m. That was my deadline.

I called NBC to see if they thought the video was a hoax. I reached out to a spokeswoman for Billy Bush and a publicist for Arianne Zucker, the soap-opera actress in the video who escorted Trump and Bush around the studio. And I reached out to Trump's spokeswoman, Hope Hicks. I sent her the transcript of the video. I asked:

"1.)Does Mr. Trump have any reason to believe that it is not authentic, and that he did not say these things? 2.) Does Mr. Trump recall that conversation? If so, does he believe there is anything that was *not* captured in this transcript that would make him look better? 3.)Does Mr. Trump have any regrets about this conversation?"

Nobody answered right away.

In the meantime, I had to start writing. The story was

easy to compose, since much of it was simply repeating what Trump had said. The only problem was the bad words.

The Post is a fairly fusty place when it comes to profanity. If a reporter tries to get a bad word into a story, the word is usually forwarded to top editors, who consider it with the gravity and speed that the Vatican applies to candidates for sainthood. That unwieldy system assumed that bad words would attack one at a time, like bad guys in a kung-fu movie.

But in this story, we were dealing with a whole army of bad words at once. The system was overloaded. When Trump said, "Grab 'em by the p----," for instance, the editors weren't sure people would be able to guess right away what "p----" was. They added a letter at the end: "p---y."

Other words required a ruling from the bosses.

"Go find out about 'tits'!" I heard one editor tell another, while the story was being edited — Trump had used the word in criticizing a woman's appearance. The second editor left to find a higher-ranking editor who could make a ruling. " 'Tits' is all right," he said when he returned.

At this point, 3:30 p.m. was getting closer.

We didn't get any on-the-record response from NBC, Bush or Zucker.

Then we heard from Trump's spokeswoman.

She'd read the transcript. She said: That doesn't sound like Mr. Trump. She wanted to see the video. We sent it to them at 3:50 p.m., with a warning that we would publish the story soon — with or without their comment.

Then nothing. Our lawyers and editors were satisfied that the tape was legitimate and newsworthy. The story was edited and ready to go. 4 p.m. arrived. Terri Rupar, the national digital editor, was walking to her desk to hit the button and publish it without comment from Trump.

I yelled for Terri to stop.

Trump was admitting it.

"This was locker room banter, a private conversation that took place many years ago. Bill Clinton has said far worse to me on the golf course — not even close. I apologize if anyone was offended," he said in a statement that arrived at that moment.

The story published at 4:02 p.m. It became the most-read story of all time on The Post's website, easily surpassing the past champion, a tale about a woman from Burundi who was believed dead but returned to crash her own funeral. At one point, more than 100,000 people were simultaneously reading the story about the video. The servers that measure The Post's Web traffic actually broke because there was too much traffic.

Afterward, Trump's deficit in polling averages increased, from a little over 3 points to more than 5 points. Prominent Republicans turned to denounce him. House Speaker Paul D. Ryan (R-Wis.) said he was "sickened."

Trump's running mate, Indiana Gov. Mike Pence, was whisked out of a campaign event — viewing a collection of autographed cardboard hot-dog buns in Toledo — without comment.

Trump himself made a second, more thorough apology in a 90-second Facebook video later that evening. "I said it, I was wrong, and I apologize," he said.

I had to buy another suit, for TV appearances. My daughter, now fully over the idea that her father was on TV, began complaining when I came on and she had to switch off "Peppa Pig." I had to quit doing the cooking at home. (Nobody complained about that.)

On Twitter I watched myself become a minor celebrity — all because of a story that had, essentially, fallen into my lap.

"My wife says that David @Fahrenthold is a time traveler from the future trying to carefully fix the darkest timeline. I believe her," wrote James Church , a professor at Austin Peay State University.

And, after I appeared on Fox News Channel to talk about the story, I heard from a man in Milwaukee. He called The Post but couldn't say "Fahrenthold" in a way that the voice-mail system recognized.

He wound up in the voice-mail box of another reporter in Sports.

"I wanna kill him," the caller said of me. "Thank you."

The Post took this seriously. I met with the D.C. police and the FBI, and a security consultant the paper hired. She was a congenial woman, a former counterterrorism official. When she arrived at our house she terrified us far more than the actual death threat had.

"Your cars are parked too far away for a car bomb," she said, looking out the front windows at the street. "They'll probably cut your brake lines." She recommended having a car patrol the neighborhood. She recommended a safe room.

She recommended stocking the safe room with provisions, in case we were under siege so long that we needed snacks.

I had to get back to work. My wife — who hadn't complained about any of this, the long hours or the missed bedtimes or the early-morning TV appearances — stopped me, shaken at what I'd gotten us into.

When the leaked Trump video still seemed to have swung the 2016 campaign, I was interviewed by a German reporter, who asked, "Do you have the feeling … 'This is it, this is the peak of my career?' "

THE POINT OF MY STORIES WAS NOT TO DEFEAT TRUMP. THE point was to tell readers the facts about this man running for president. How reliable was he at keeping promises? How much moral responsibility did he feel to help those less fortunate than he?

By the end of the election, I felt I'd done my job. My last big story about Trump started with an amazing anecdote, which came from a tip from a reader. In 1996, Trump had crashed a ribbon-cutting ceremony for a charity opening a nursery school for children with AIDS. Trump, who had never donated to the charity, stole a seat onstage that had been saved for a big contributor.

He sat there through the whole ceremony, singing along with the choir of children as cameras snapped, and then left without giving a dime.

"All of this is completely consistent with who Trump is," Tony Schwartz, Trump's co-author on his 1987 book "The Art of the Deal," told me. "He's a man who operates inside a tiny bubble that never extends beyond what he believes is his self-interest."

"If your worldview is only you — if all you're seeing is a

mirror — then there's nobody to give money to," Schwartz said. "Except yourself."

ELECTION DAY CAME. I THOUGHT MY TIME WITH TRUMP had come to an end.

That night, my job was to co-write the main Web story about the election. My colleague Matea Gold and I were supposed to pre-write stories for all the likely outcomes. I volunteered to write the one that said "Trump wins."

Based on the polling data, it felt fantastical and point-less, like designing a Super Bowl ring for the Cleveland Browns.

"Biggest upset of the modern era?" I asked Post polit-ical reporter Dan Balz, trying to use the right tone in this story that nobody would ever read. Balz said that was right.

Then the polls started to close.

And it turned out that I am not a time traveler.

About 10 p.m., as the tide turned against Clinton, the editors started killing or reshaping stories they had assigned hours before. They axed CLINTON, a story about the history Clinton would make as the first woman to win the White House. They ordered a rewrite of GOP, which was supposed to tell readers how — with Trump defeated — the GOP was licking its wounds and looking ahead to 2020. Across the newsroom, paragraphs were being deleted en masse. An entire presupposed version of the future was disappearing. It wasn't the future after all.

Finally, at 2:32 a.m., the Associated Press called Wisconsin.

Donald Trump holds a mask depicting himself during a campaign event in Sarasota, Fla., on Nov. 7, 2016. (Jabin Botsford/The Washington Post)

Trump was over the top.

"PUB TRUMP WINS STORY," I wrote to the editors, giving the order to publish the story I'd written earlier.

"Donald John Trump has been projected as the winner of the presidential election, according to the Associated Press. … His victory on Tuesday was the biggest surprise of the modern presidential era. …"

THAT NIGHT, I ARRIVED HOME ABOUT 4 A.M. TO A QUIET house. I found a stale beer in the back of the fridge.

In the past, I'd always been able to step out of my job at times like this.

No matter how big the day's story was, there was always

a bigger world, which was still spinning unaffected by the murder I'd covered in Northeast Washington or the natural disaster or the congressional vote I'd just witnessed. But this story was too big to step out of.

As I sat on the couch with my nasty pale ale, it occurred to me that I would be living *in* the story, from that point on.

A few days later, I was interviewed by another German reporter. He asked if these past nine months, the greatest adventure in my life as a journalist, had been for naught.

"Do you feel like your work perhaps did not matter at all?" he said.

I didn't feel like that.

It *did* matter. But, in an election as long and wild as this, a lot of other stories and other people mattered, too. I did my job. The voters did theirs. Now my job goes on. I'll seek to cover Trump the president with the same vigor as I scrutinized Trump the candidate.

And now I know how to do it.

THE STORIES

David Fahrenthold ✔
@Fahrenthold

After inquiries by the Post, Trump details how much of the $6M he raised for vets he has actually been given away.

What ever happened to all that money Trump raised for the veterans?
The campaign says half of the $6 million has gone to charities, but some are asking about the rest.
washingtonpost.com

RETWEETS	LIKES	
2	3	

4:40 PM - 3 Mar 2016

↩   🔁 2   ♥ 3

What ever happened to all that money Trump raised for the veterans?

By David A. Fahrenthold
March 3, 2016

In January, Donald Trump skipped a televised Republican debate in Iowa and held his own event instead — a rally to raise money for veterans. Trump said it was a huge success.

"One hour. Six million dollars," Trump told a campaign rally in Iowa a few days later, boasting about the total raised. He listed more than 20 groups that would receive money. "These people that get these checks are amazing people, amazing people."

More than a month later, about half of the money, roughly $3 million, has been donated to veterans' charities, according to a summary released Thursday by the Trump campaign in response to inquiries from The Washington Post.

Republican presidential candidate Donald Trump, shown at a campaign event Tuesday at the Mar-a-Lago Club in Palm Beach, Fla., said he raised $6 million for veterans groups at a January fundraiser. (Jabin Botsford/The Washington Post)

In recent days, after the campaign initially did not provide details of where the money had gone, The Post had undertaken its own accounting. After contacting each of the 24 charities that Trump had previously listed as his beneficiaries, The Post had accounted for less than half of the $6 million.

Hope Hicks, a spokeswoman for Trump's campaign, said Trump still intended to give the rest of the money away to veterans groups. She also criticized the news media for repeated inquiries into what became of the funds.

"If the media spent half as much time highlighting the work of these groups and how our veterans have been so mistreated, rather than trying to disparage Mr. Trump's generosity for a totally unsolicited gesture for which he had no obligation, we would all be better for it," Hicks wrote in an email.

Trump's fundraiser highlighted the billionaire presidential candidate's remarkable ability to draw people, attention and money to any cause he chooses. Trump enticed enormous gifts from wealthy friends, including Stewart Rahr, a colorful New York philanthropist who calls himself "Stewie Rah Rah, the Number One King of All Fun." Their money became life-altering gifts for some small charities, which received $50,000 or $100,000 each.

But the aftermath of that event showed another side of Trump's campaign: its tendency to focus on front-end spectacle over back-end details. The rollout of contributions has raised questions about how long Trump would keep donated funds within the Donald J. Trump Foundation, a personal charity whose gifts can boost his political brand.

"Where's the rest of the money going?" said Keith David at the Task Force Dagger Foundation, which offers support to Special Operations personnel and their families.

David's group typifies the confusion over Trump's money. It was listed by Trump as a group that would benefit from his fundraising. And soon after the Iowa fundraising event, the group got a check for $50,000. It came from Rahr's foundation, with a note that mentioned Trump.

But was that it? The group's board — noting the huge amount of money that Trump raised and the lesser amount of money Trump seemed to have given out — decided it could not be.

"There's a large chunk missing. I'm just kind of curious as to where that money went," David said. "I'd like to see some of it come to us, because we are on the list."

The list, as given out by Trump's campaign Thursday, does not show any more donations going for David's group.

Trump's veterans fundraiser was, if nothing else, a smart bit of political theater.

It allowed Trump, who was feuding with Fox News Channel at the time, to boycott a GOP debate that Fox was hosting — and, at the same time, claim both the moral high ground and a prime-time TV spotlight for himself that competed directly with the debate he was skipping.

"We set up the website. I called some friends. And the sign was just given: We just cracked $6 million," Trump said, savoring the moment at the end. He announced that the money would be divided among more than 20 veterans' groups: "They're going to get a lot of money. Everybody is going to get a lot of money," he said.

Some of that money was raised from small donors online, at the website donaldtrumpforvets.com. That site now says it has raised $1.67 million.

But the bulk of the $6 milllion was raised from a small group of Trump's very wealthy friends.

Not all of them gave in the same way.

Billionaire investor Carl Icahn gave $500,000 and sent it directly to two groups: a charity to help Army Green Berets and another for Navy SEALs. Another $1 million came from Rahr.

Trump offered Rahr a menu of veterans' charities, Rahr associate Steve Burns said in an email. Rahr chose 11, based on a review of "missions and financials. We felt they were the best ones in helping the vets," Burns said.

The $1.5 million in donations from Icahn and Rahr, which bypassed the Trump Foundation, are easy to track.

Associates of the two men said they have given the money directly to the charities, and multiple charities said they had received it.

But other benefactors gave their money to the Trump Foundation, so Trump could divvy it up himself. One was Phil Ruffin, a Las Vegas casino mogul, who gave $1 million. "He trusts Mr. Trump to make that decision," a spokeswoman said.

In all, Trump's campaign said the Trump Foundation had given out about $1.1 million so far. Hicks, Trump's campaign spokeswoman, did not immediately respond to a question about how much of the money raised for veterans remains in the accounts of the Trump Foundation.

In the days that followed the Iowa fundraiser, the donations — ostensibly, apolitical gifts to needy veterans — became a centerpiece of Trump's campaign rallies. He would frequently call the leaders of local charities up onstage and hand them a huge check in front of the cameras and the crowds.

"I thought I was going to faint, because we had no idea — until that check came up on the stage — we had no idea what we were getting," said Cindy Brodie of Partners for Patriots, which trains service dogs to help veterans with disabilities.

At the time of Trump's fundraiser, Brodie and her husband had been struggling to keep themselves and the charity afloat. But then a veteran whom they had helped met Trump at a campaign event elsewhere in Iowa.

And then Brodie was being called up onstage by the billionaire and handed an oversized $100,000 check.

But — after the campaign moved on from Iowa —

Trump's donations seemed to lag behind his promises. In early February, the Wall Street Journalreported that many groups began to get their checks only after the Journal asked the Trump campaign why they had not.

Trump's figures show the biggest beneficiary was the Navy SEAL Foundation, a Virginia-based group that helps Navy Special Operations forces and their families. It received $450,000, according to Trump's campaign. The Green Beret Foundation, which helps Army Special Forces soldiers and their families, got $350,000. Two other groups got $200,000. Fourteen charities got $100,000 each. Six got $50,000 each, and two others got less.

"Our budget is, like, $40,000 a year," said Sarah Petersen, the founder of Support Siouxland Soldiers, which provides emergency relief to homeless or near-homeless veterans in Iowa. Trump gave the group $100,000. "Our largest donation was $10,000. So this is a pretty big deal for us."

Hicks, the spokeswoman for Trump's campaign, declined to give details about how the rest of the money would be handed out.

"We will continue to allocate contributions to groups that have been announced," Hicks said, "as well as additional groups that are being considered."

What additional groups?

Hicks could only name one: a Queens-based nonprofit called Veterans-in-Command, which provides housing, food and job counseling to veterans. In that case, the Trump Foundation dipped into its veterans funds to present a donation.

Which happened to solve a political headache for Trump himself.

At the time of the donation, the New York media was mocking Trump for mishandling a past request the group had made for a donation. Instead of money, the Trump campaign had sent them Trump bumper stickers.

"He called us, and he apologized, and he did the right thing by us," said Larry Robertson, the Queens group's president. Trump paid off some old debts and paid for one year's rent on a new office, a total gift worth about $26,200.

That was 0.4 percent of the money Trump said he'd raised for veterans. The Queens group is hoping it is the beginning, not the end, of a relationship.

"We're going to have a grand opening. Hopefully he's going to be here," Robertson said in a telephone interview. "It's going to be about another week. He'll be here.

David Fahrenthold ✔
@Fahrenthold

Trump says he's given $102M to charity. He meant: free rounds of golf, land easements, but no gifts of his own $.

Missing from Trump's list of charitable giving: His own personal cash

List of billionaire's charitable donations over the past 5 years shows a giving style that appears tailored to his own interests rather than lofty philanthropic ambitions.

washingtonpost.com

RETWEETS LIKES
934   674

  ethix

8:07 PM - 10 Apr 2016

↩ 122   ↻ 934   ♥ 674

Missing from Trump's list of charitable giving: His own personal cash

By David A. Fahrenthold and Rosalind S. Helderman
April 10, 2016

Since the first day of his presidential campaign, Donald Trump has said that he gave more than $102 million to charity in the past five years.

To back up that claim, Trump's campaign compiled a list of his contributions— 4,844 of them, filling 93 pages.

But, in that massive list, one thing was missing.

Not a single one of those donations was actually a personal gift of Trump's own money.

Instead, according to a Washington Post analysis, many of the gifts that Trump cited to prove his generosity were free rounds of golf, given away by his courses for charity auctions and raffles.

The largest items on the list were not cash gifts but

Donations to the Donald J. Trump Foundation

Donald Trump often uses the Donald J. Trump Foundation to make gifts to friends' charities and to donate to groups that do business at his clubs and hotels. But its funding has largely been provided by other people.

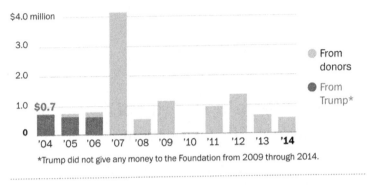

* Trump did not give any money to the Foundation from 2009 through 2014.

TOP DONORS, 2004-2014

Vince and Linda McMahon
World Wrestling Entertainment — $5 million

Donald J. Trump — $2 million

Richard Ebers
Inside Sports and Entertainment — $1.9 million

NBC Universal Media
Aired "The Apprentice" show — $500,000

Comedy Central
Aired a roast of Trump — $400,000

Note: 2014 is the last year for which tax records are available

Source: Washington Post analysis of Donald J. Trump Foundation tax records

DAVID FAHRENTHOLD AND CRISTINA RIVERO/THE WASHINGTON POST

land-conservation agreements to forgo development rights on property Trump owns.

Trump's campaign also counted a parcel of land that he'd given to New York state — although that was in 2006, not within the past five years.

In addition, many of the gifts on the list came from the charity that bears his name, the Donald J. Trump

Foundation, which didn't receive a personal check from Trump from 2009 through 2014, according to the most recent public tax filings. Its work is largely funded by others, although Trump decides where the gifts go.

Some beneficiaries on the list are not charities at all: They included clients, other businesses and tennis superstar Serena Williams.

This list produced by Trump's campaign — which has not been reported in detail before — provides an unusually broad portrait of Trump's giving, and his approach to philanthropy in general.

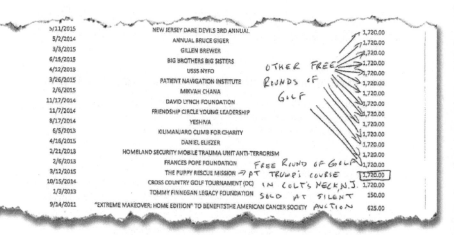

This page, from Trump's 93-page list of charitable contributions shows free rounds of golf. In all, Trump claimed credit for 2,900 free rounds given away at his club.

It reveals how Trump has demonstrated less of the soaring, world-changing ambitions in his philanthropy than many other billionaires. Instead, his giving appears narrowly tied to his business and, now, his political interests.

His foundation, for example, frequently gave money to groups that paid to use Trump's facilities, and it donated to conservatives who could help promote Trump's rise in the Republican Party. The foundation's second-biggest donation described on the campaign's list went to the charity of a man who had settled a lawsuit with one of Trump's golf courses after being denied a hole-in-one prize.

The tally of Trump's giving was provided by Trump's campaign last year to the Associated Press, which was attempting to assess Trump's recent record of charitable giving. The AP, which did not publish the list, provided it to The Post.

When asked about The Post's analysis, a top Trump aide acknowledged that none of the gifts had come in cash

Donald Trump's charitable giving, according to Trump

In a 93-page document compiled by the Trump campaign, Trump laid out the transactions that accounted for his boast of more than $102 million in charitable giving over five years. None of the items on the list are cash gifts from Trump himself.

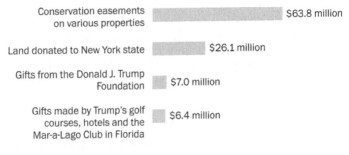

LARGEST CHARITABLE GIFTS, 2010-2014

Conservation easements on various properties	$63.8 million
Land donated to New York state	$26.1 million
Gifts from the Donald J. Trump Foundation	$7.0 million
Gifts made by Trump's golf courses, hotels and the Mar-a-Lago Club in Florida	$6.4 million

Note: 2014 is the last year for which tax records are available

Source: Washington Post analysis of Donald J. Trump Foundation tax records

DAVID FAHRENTHOLD AND CRISTINA RIVERO/THE WASHINGTON POST

from the billionaire himself. But, he said, that was because the list was not a complete account of Trump's gifts.

The aide, Allen Weisselberg, chief financial officer of the Trump Organization, said Trump had, in fact, given generously from his own pocket. But Weisselberg declined to provide any documentation, such as saying how much charitable giving Trump has declared in his federal tax filings.

"We want to keep them quiet," said Weisselberg, who is also treasurer of the Trump Foundation. "He doesn't want other charities to see it. Then it becomes like a feeding frenzy."

'THE GRATEFUL MILLIONAIRE'

In the early years of his career — when Trump was making a name as America's human embodiment of success — he was known for acts of real, and well-publicized, philanthropy.

In 1986, Trump heard about a Georgia farmer who'd committed suicide because of an impending foreclosure. He reached out.

"He said, 'Forget it. I'll pay it off.' He paid for it out of his personal money," said Betsy Sharp, the daughter of the farmer, Leonard Hill III. Trump flew the family to Trump Tower to burn the hated mortgage in front of TV cameras, with an ebony cigarette lighter that said "New York."

Through a combination of good deeds and good publicity, the idea of Trump as a gallant friend of the little guy caught on. By the late 1990s, as documented by the debunking site Snopes.com, Trump's name had been grafted onto a classic American urban legend, known to folklorists as "The Grateful Millionaire."

Trump — it was said in email chains and books of inspirational stories — had once been stranded in a limo. A good Samaritan stopped to help. Trump secretly paid off his mortgage. The legend goes back to at least 1954, when the grateful millionaire was Henry Ford.

The most complete public accounting of Trump's actual charity so far is the $102 million list provided by his campaign last year, titled "Donald J. Trump Charitable Contributions."

In places, it appears to be an unedited mash-up of internal lists kept by Trump's golf clubs, noting all the things they'd given away to anybody. True charities like the National Center for Missing and Exploited Children are followed by freebies given away at sales meetings, followed by entries in cryptic internal shorthand. At a Trump golf

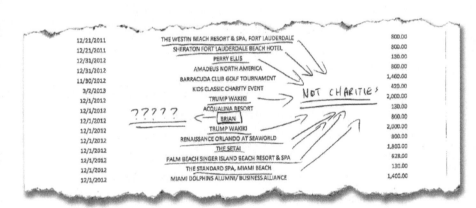

This page of "charitable contributions" from Trump's course in Miami seems to show giveaways to for-profit businesses, and a man named Brian.

course in Miami, for instance, the recipient of a $800 gift was listed only as "Brian."

To identify what the gifts represented, The Post interviewed recipients to find out what they'd received — and matched those gifts to others with the exact same dollar value.

By extrapolation, The Post estimated that Trump claimed credit for at least 2,900 free rounds of golf, 175 free hotel stays, 165 free meals and 11 gift certificates to spas.

"I thought it would be a pretty hot ticket, [and] it was," said Marion Satterthwaite, who runs a charity that helps bring back dogs that U.S. service members have bonded with overseas. She was holding a silent auction, and one of things she auctioned off was a free round of golf donated by Trump's private golf club in Colts Neck, N.J. At that club, Trump appeared to claim donations of 76 foursomes, each valued at $1,720. Satterthwaite said that, in her case, it sold for less.

But Trump's list was also riddled with apparent errors, in which the "charities" that got his gifts didn't seem to be charities at all.

Trump listed a donation to "Serena William Group" in February 2015, valued at exactly $1,136.56. A spokeswoman for the tennis star said she had attended a ribbon-cutting at Trump's Loudoun County, Va., golf course that year for a new tennis center. But Trump hadn't donated to her charity. Instead, he had given her a free ride from Florida on his plane and a free framed photo of herself.

The Post sent an annotated version of this list — showing the results of its analysis, and its extrapolations about

10/31/2014	JILL'S HOUSE	80.00
2/28/2015	LANGLEY SCHOOL	80.00
3/31/2015	WOMEN AND WINE EVENT	80.00
3/31/2015	WOMEN AND WINE EVENT	80.00
6/30/2014	WOMEN'S GOLF ASSOCIATION MAD HATTER EVENT	125.00
2/25/2015	FIRST TEE OF DC	5,744.00
2/26/2015	SERENA WILLIAM GROUP	1,136.56
7/12/2010	AMERICAN RED CROSS LONG BEACH CHAPTER	591.26
8/19/2010	ANTI-DEFAMATION LEAGUE	591.26
6/17/2010	ASIAN BUSINESS LEAGUE	591.26
7/16/2010	ASIAN PACIFIC COMMUNITY FUND GALA	591.26
5/14/2010	ASIAN SOCIETY	591.26
3/23/2010	BOYS & GIRLS CLUBS LA	1,182.52
5/6/2010	BRIGHTER FUTURES FOR KIDS	591.26
9/17/2010	CABRILLO MARINE AQUARIUM	591.26

This page, from Trump's course in Virginia, appears to count as 'charity' gifts given to visiting VIP Serena Williams. Williams says she got a free plane ride and a framed photo of herself.

what each gift represented — to the Trump campaign, along with a detailed list of questions about Trump's giving.

The Trump campaign declined to answer most of the questions or to provide an interview with Trump.

The Post's analysis showed that the small giveaways from Trump businesses seemed to account for the bulk of the 4,844 transactions that Trump took credit for. But they accounted for only about $6.4 million of the total dollar figure.

The most expensive charitable contributions on Trump's list, by contrast, dealt with transactions related to real estate.

For one, Trump counted $63.8 million of unspecified "conservation easements." That refers to legal arrangements — which could bring tax breaks — in which a landowner agrees to forgo certain kinds of development on land that he owns. In California, for example, Trump agreed to an easement that prevented him from building homes on a plot of land near a golf course. But Trump kept the land, and kept making money off it. It is a driving range.

In this election, neither of Trump's Republican rivals — Sen. Ted Cruz (Tex.) nor Ohio Gov. John Kasich — has detailed his recent charitable giving. Among the Democrats, former secretary of state Hillary Clinton said she and her husband gave 11 percent of their yearly income, and the Clintons have also established a foundation that has collected $2 billion for charity around the world, while also increasing their global celebrity and political network. Sen. Bernie Sanders (Vt.) said he gave 5 percent of his yearly income.

Trump has not entirely given up making splashy public gifts.

In 2009, for instance, Trump appeared on the TV show "Extra" and promised that he would pay a struggling viewer's bills. "This is really a bad time for a lot of people," Trump said as the contest was announced.

The winner, who got $5,000, was a woman who runs a spray-tanning business.

But the contest's rules, posted online, made clear that the winner would not be flown to New York like the family Trump helped in the 1980s. Moreover, the rules said, the winner would have to pay for cab fare.

"The winner must live in New York, provide their own transportation to Trump Tower, and be willing to meet Donald on-camera to accept his check," the rules warned.

According to tax records, the winner's check came from the Donald J. Trump Foundation, the charity created by Trump in the late 1980s. The same was true on Saturday, when Trump made a well-publicized $100,000 gift to the

National September 11 Memorial Museum in New York. The foundation gave the money after Trump made a brief visit to the museum as he campaigned ahead of next week's New York primary.

THE TRUMP FOUNDATION

On the $102 million list created by Trump's campaign, he claims credit for $7 million given by the foundation, where Trump serves as president.

The biggest donors to his foundation in recent years have been other people, most notably Vince and Linda McMahon, top executives at World Wrestling Entertainment. They donated $5 million after Trump made a cameo on "Wrestlemania" in 2007, according to a spokesman for WWE. The spokesman said Trump was paid separately for the appearance. Linda McMahon has since left WWE and is now active in politics. She and her husband both declined to comment about the donation.

Trump's foundation has operated on a smaller scale than some run by his billionaire peers. Filmmaker George Lucas, for instance, who is tied with Trump at 324th place in Forbes's list of the world's billionaires, donated $925 million to his family foundation in 2012. In 2014, Lucas's foundation gave out $55 million in donations to museums, hospitals, artistic groups and environmental charities.

Media magnate Sumner Redstone, also tied with Trump in the Forbes rankings, gave $28 million from his company to his foundation that year, and the foundation in turn gave out $31 million in gifts.

The Trump Foundation gave out $591,000 in 2014.

"He's using [the foundation] as a kind of checkbook, with other people's money," Leslie Lenkowsky, a faculty member at Indiana University's school of philanthropy, said after The Post described the recipients of the Trump Foundation's gifts.

"Not a good model. It's not wrong. It's not unique. But it's poor philanthropy."

In 2013, Trump was trying to persuade the V Foundation — a cancer-fighting group founded by Jim Valvano, the college basketball coach who died in 1993 — to hold a fundraiser at his Trump Winery in Virginia.

Trump's foundation gave $10,000 to the V Foundation that summer, just when the V Foundation later said it was being wooed. He got the fundraiser.

Trump's foundation also gave to the American Cancer Society, the Dana-Farber Cancer Institute and the Leukemia and Lymphoma Society, all of which have held fundraisers at his Mar-a-Lago Club in Palm Beach, Fla.

In 2010, a man named Martin Greenberg was playing in a charity tournament at Trump's course in Briarcliff Manor, N.Y. A $1 million prize was offered to anybody who got a hole in one.

Greenberg did. But then, hours later, he was called back. The rules said the hole-in-one shot had to go 150 yards. But, according to court documents, Trump's course had made the hole too short.

Greenberg got nothing. He sued.

On the day that Trump and the other parties told the court that they had settled the case, the Donald J. Trump Foundation made its first and only donation to the Martin

B. Greenberg Foundation, for $158,000. Both Greenberg and Trump's campaign declined to comment.

Trump also used the foundation's money to play the role of a big-hearted billionaire on TV — doling out at least $194,000 to various causes favored by contestants on "Celebrity Apprentice," Trump's spinoff reality show that appeared on NBC.

In 2012, NBC Universal made a $500,000 donation to the Trump Foundation. NBC Universal declined to comment about that gift.

In some cases, the recipient was a complete stranger: a club member who stopped him at the pool, another golfer, or a woman who'd just walked into his office.

"I'll never forget. He said, 'Debra, you have the 'it' factor. He said, 'I don't know any other beautiful woman going into the inner city,' " said Debra George, a Christian minister in Texas who met Trump when a mutual friend brought her along to his office. Trump asked how she paid for her work.

"It's kind of like walking on air. We trust God," she told him. "He said, 'I'm going to help you.'" Trump's foundation gave her charity $10,000.

Some recipients said they liked the Trump Foundation's informal approach to giving. "(At) a lot of foundations, you know, there's a grant process," said Barbara Abernathy, whose charity helps children with cancer. Not Trump, whom Abernathy had met at a Mar-a-Lago gala. She later asked his people for money, to help a patient's family afford medicine and a car payment. She got $1,000 in two weeks."

In 2013, Scott K. York, then the head of the Board of Supervisors in Loudoun County, came to Trump's son to ask for help. An elementary school in the county needed a $110,000 handicapped-accessible playground. York asked for $10,000. Trump's foundation gave $7,500.

A month later, the Trump Foundation gave $50,000 to the American Conservative Union Foundation. With donations to that group, Politico has reported, Trump was building a relationship that won him prime speaking slots at the Conservative Political Action Conference, a coveted venue for an aspiring Republican presidential candidate.

In this campaign, Trump said he brought in more than $6 million during a fundraiser for veterans groups he held on Jan. 28 in Iowa.

But the Trump campaign has detailed only about $3 million worth of donations that have been given to veterans groups. Some were given directly by donors recruited by Trump, and in some cases, the Trump Foundation served as a middleman.

Trump's campaign has said that Trump is continuing to identify and vet new recipients for the money but declined to provide additional details.

Trump spokeswoman Hope Hicks declined to respond to questions regarding whether Trump has followed through on a pledge to donate $1 million of his own money to the cause.

Still, as he has campaigned, Trump has benefited from a reputation for generosity.

"His limousine broke down one time, a couple stopped and helped him. He paid off their mortgage a few days later. These are all things that you never hear about Donald Trump," Jerry Falwell Jr., the president of Liberty University, said on Fox News's "Hannity" in January.

The Grateful Millionaire. The legend, alive and well.

In a telephone interview, Falwell, who has endorsed Trump, was asked: Did you ever ask Trump if that story was true?

"I never did," Falwell said. "But, Trey, didn't you search that on Google?"

"I didn't," his son Trey said. "But somebody did."

"It was in some publication in 1995," the elder Falwell concluded. "But I forget which publication."

Anu Narayanswamy and Alice Crites contributed to this report.

David Fahrenthold ✓
@Fahrenthold

Following ⌄

Thx all who RTd my pleas for vets who got @realdonaldtrump's $ yest'day. We couldn't find 'em b/c they didn't exist.

Four months after fundraiser, Trump says he gave $1 million to veterans group
The timing of Trump's gift contradicts statements from his campaign and comes as the GOP candidate is under fire for his accounting of a veterans' fundraiser he hel...
washingtonpost.com

RETWEETS	LIKES	
336	336	

4:50 PM - 24 May 2016

↩ 33   ⟲ 336   ♥ 336

Four months after fundraiser, Trump says he gave $1 million to veterans group

By David A. Fahrenthold
May 24, 2016

ALMOST FOUR MONTHS AFTER PROMISING $1 MILLION OF his own money to veterans' causes, Donald Trump moved to fulfill that pledge Monday evening — promising the entire sum to a single charity as he came under intense media scrutiny.

Trump, now the presumptive Republican presidential nominee, organized a nationally televised fundraiser for veterans' causes in Des Moines on Jan. 28. That night, Trump said he had raised $6 million, including the gift from his own pocket.

"Donald Trump gave $1 million," he said then.

As recently as last week, Trump's campaign manager had insisted that the mogul had already given that money away. But that was false: Trump had not.

In recent days, The Washington Post and other media outlets had pressed Trump and his campaign for details about how much the fundraiser had actually raised and whether Trump had given his portion.

The candidate refused to provide details. On Monday, a Post reporter used Twitter — Trump's preferred social-media platform — to search publicly for any veterans groups that had received Trump's money.

By Monday afternoon, The Post had found none. But it seems to have caught the candidate's attention.

Later Monday evening, Trump called the home of James K. Kallstrom, a former FBI official who is chairman of the Marine Corps-Law Enforcement Foundation. The charity aids families of fallen Marines and federal law enforcement officers.

Trump told Kallstrom that he would give the entire $1 million to the group, according to Kallstrom's wife. Sue Kallstrom said she was not sure whether the money had been transferred yet.

Other big donors to Trump's fundraiser had already made their gifts weeks before. Why had Trump waited so long?

"You have a lot of vetting to do," Trump said Tuesday in a telephone interview conducted while he was flying to a campaign rally in Albuquerque.

For this particular donation, it would seem that little new vetting was required because Trump already knew the recipient well. The Marine Corps-Law Enforcement Foundation had already received more than $230,000 in donations from the Donald J. Trump Foundation — a charity controlled by Trump but largely funded by others. Last year, the group gave Trump its "Commandant's Leadership Award" at a gala in New York.

When asked Tuesday whether he had given the money this week only because reporters had been asking about it, Trump responded: "You know, you're a nasty guy. You're really a nasty guy. I gave out millions of dollars that I had no obligation to do."

Trump's call on Monday night stood in contradiction to an account given Friday by campaign manager Corey Lewandowski. "The money is fully spent," Lewandowski said then. "Mr. Trump's money is fully spent."

On Tuesday, Trump said Lewandowski would not have been in a position to know that. "I don't know that Corey would even know when I gave it out," he said.

In the same interview, Trump said the fundraiser had raised about $5.5 million for veterans overall. He said he was not sure how much of it remained to be given away.

That also contrasted with the account last week from Lewandowski, who said that about $4.5 million had been raised and that Trump's effort had fallen short of the promised $6 million because some unnamed big donors had backed out.

On Tuesday, Trump said no major contributors had reneged. "For the most part, I think they all came through," he said. "Some of them came through very late."

Trump also said he had never actually promised that the fundraiser had raised $6 million. "I didn't say six," he said.

But, in video of the event, Trump tells the crowd, "We just cracked $6 million! Right? $6 million."

Trump was told that he did, indeed, say "$6 million."

"Well, I don't, I don't have the notes. I don't have the tape of it," he said. "Play [the tape] for me. Because I'd like to hear it." Before the video could be cued up, Trump had moved on.

The story of his nighttime gift seemed to highlight a unique quality of Trump: his acute sensitivity to losing face on social media. He had routinely rejected questions about the fundraiser for veterans if they were posed in person.

"Why should I give you records?" Trump said in an interview with The Post earlier this month, when he was asked about the money. "I don't have to give you records."

Then, on Monday, a Post reporter publicly queried multiple veterans groups on Twitter, asking whether they had received personal donations from Trump. None had.

Hours later, after 10:38 p.m. Eastern time, Trump responded on Twitter: "While under no obligation to do so, I have raised between 5 & 6 million dollars, including 1 million dollars from me, for our VETERANS. Nice!"

And sometime that same evening, Trump called to make the donation to James Kallstrom's group. Sue Kallstrom wasn't sure what time the call was, only that it happened after she went to bed at 8 p.m.

"I guess he wants to take care of the vets," she said. Among its other good works, the foundation provides $30,000 educational grants to the children of the fallen. "The foundation is thrilled, because the [money] is going to help a lot of people. Especially the children."

Trump's campaign has said the remainder of the donations would be given out by Memorial Day. Trump said he would ask his staff to send The Post a list of the groups that would receive that money, but his staff did not immediately provide it.

But it did appear that Trump's staff was preparing to disburse more gifts. In Boston on Tuesday, the founder of the city's annual Wounded Vet Bike Run got a call.

"For some reason, a Trump campaign worker reached out to me today and asked for our nonprofit number, and I gave it to 'em," said Andrew Biggio, the group's founder.

The annual motorcycle ride raises money to help veterans and their families, including giving away cars and retrofitting motorcycles for the disabled. He said the staffer did not tell him how much money to expect. "I have no idea what's coming down the pike," Biggio said.

In recent weeks, other veterans groups had been struggling to figure out how to ask for some of Trump's remaining money. Trump had provided no formal way to apply.

Biggio said he had not formally applied but was pretty sure how he had come to be on Trump's radar.

"I served in Iraq with Donald Trump's bodyguard's son," he said.

Jose A. DelReal contributed to this report.

David Fahrenthold ✓
@Fahrenthold

`Following` ⌄

UPDATE @realDonaldTrump says he gives millions of his own $ to charity. I've tried 157 charities w/ties to him &...

TO CHARITY BY DONALD
TRUMP BETWEEN 1/1/09
AND 5/23/16

*1) 2009, DONATION TO POLICE ATHLETIC LEAGUE
OF NYC. AMOUNT $5,000 to $9,999

* May be a book-keeping error.

RETWEETS   LIKES
326   338

1:01 PM - 27 Jun 2016

Trump promised millions to charity. We found less than $10,000 over 7 years.

By David A. Fahrenthold
June 28, 2016

In May, under pressure from the news media, Donald Trump made good on a pledge he made four months earlier: He gave $1 million to a nonprofit group helping veterans' families.

Before that, however, when was the last time that Trump had given any of his own money to a charity?

If Trump stands by his promises, such donations should be occurring all the time. In the 15 years prior to the veterans donation, Trump promised to donate earnings from a wide variety of his moneymaking enterprises: "The Apprentice." Trump Vodka. Trump University. A book. Another book. If he had honored all those pledges, Trump's gifts to charity would have topped $8.5 million.

But in the 15 years prior to the veterans' gift, public

records show that Trump donated about $2.8 million through a foundation set up to give his money away — less than a third of the pledged amount — and nothing since 2009. Records show Trump has given nothing to his foundation since 2008.

Trump and his staff are adamant that he has given away millions privately, off the foundation's books. Trump won't release his tax returns, which would confirm such gifts, and his staff won't supply details. "There's no way for you to know or understand," Trump spokeswoman Hope Hicks told BuzzFeed recently.

Hicks did not respond to repeated questions about Trump's charity from The Washington Post. Trump earlier this month revoked The Post's press credentials to cover his events.

In recent weeks, The Post tried to answer the question by digging up records going back to the late 1980s and canvassing a wide swath of nonprofits with some connection to Trump.

That research showed that Trump has a long-standing habit of promising to give to charity. But Trump's follow-through on those promises was middling — even at the beginning, in his early days as a national celebrity.

In the 1980s, Trump pledged to give away royalties from his first book to fight AIDS and multiple sclerosis. But he gave less to those causes than he did to his older daughter's ballet school.

In recent years, Trump's follow-through on his promises has been seemingly nonexistent.

The Post contacted 188 charities searching for evidence of personal gifts from Trump in the period between 2008 and this May. The Post sought out charities that had some link to Trump, either because he had given them his foundation's money, appeared at their charity galas or praised them publicly.

The search turned up just one donation in that period — a 2009 gift of between $5,000 and $9,999 to the Police Athletic League of New York City.

'AN AGENT FOR CHARITIES'

In all, when the $1 million gift to veterans is added to his giving through the Donald J. Trump Foundation, Trump has given at least $3.8 million to charity since 2001. That is a significant sum, although not among billionaires. For example, hedge-fund titan Stanley Druckenmiller, just behind Trump on Forbes's rankings of net worth, gave $120 million to his foundation in 2013 alone.

What has set Trump apart from other wealthy philanthropists is not how much he gives — it is how often he promises that he is *going* to give.

From 1988: "To the homeless, to Vietnam veterans, for AIDS, multiple sclerosis," Trump said about proceeds from his first book, "The Art of the Deal." "Originally, I figured they'd get a couple of hundred thousand, but because of the success of 'The Art of the Deal,' they'll get four or five million."

From 2015: "The profits of my book?" Trump said when a reporter asked about what he would do with the proceeds from his most recent book, "Crippled America." "I'm giving them away, to a lot of different — including the vets. 'Kay?"

These promises seemed designed to reassure potential customers and voters and to reconcile two sides of Trump's public persona. On one hand, Trump said he had so much money that he didn't need more. But on the other hand, he was always selling something.

The explanation was that the money Trump was making wasn't for him to keep.

"I am acting as an agent for charities," Trump said in 1989 at the unveiling of Trump: The Game. In news accounts, he estimated the board game alone would bring in $20 million for charity.

Milton Bradley, which made the game, saw the need for such a promise firsthand. After the company released the game — a Monopoly-like board game with Trump branding — it didn't sell.

"The game was just nailed to the shelf," said George DiTomassi, who was president of Milton Bradley at the time. One problem, he said, was that customers were not told about Trump's pledge to give proceeds to charity. "They felt perhaps this was going to be something that a millionaire would make some money on," DiTomassi said.

The TV commercial for the product was changed. "Mr. Trump's proceeds from Trump: The Game will be donated to charity," a new voice-over said at the end.

It still didn't work. The game tanked.

Still, Trump said he made $880,000 from it, and even more from "The Art of the Deal." In 1987, the mogul started the Donald J. Trump Foundation to donate his royalties.

But the proceeds didn't go straight to charity. They went straight into Trump's bank account.

"Are you asking me whether or not I took the check … and endorsed it over to a charity?" Trump said on the witness stand in a 1991 New York state court case, brought by a man who accused him of stealing the idea for Trump: The Game. "Who would ever do that?"

Trump said he did eventually pass money to his foundation, which gave it away to charities. He said he had given away even more than he had earned.

But when Trump ran into financial troubles in the middle of 1990, records show that his giving to the foundation slowed — then stopped. In 1991, he gave no money to the foundation. If book and game royalties came in that year, Trump apparently found another use for them.

When Trump did give his money to charities, it wasn't always to the well-known causes he mentioned in interviews.

One case in point was the promise, made in the promotion of "The Art of the Deal," that Trump would give royalties "to the homeless, to Vietnam veterans, for AIDS, multiple sclerosis."

He did give to those causes — but not very much.

From 1987 to 1991, Trump gave away $1.9 million of his money through the Donald J. Trump Foundation.

He gave $101,000 to veterans, according to a Post analysis of tax records from that time.

He gave $26,000 to the homeless.

He gave $12,450 to AIDS charities.

He gave $4,250 to multiple-sclerosis research.

The amount for those categories was $143,700, or nearly 8 percent of the total.

Much of the rest went to charities tied to Trump's life:

```
*AIDS CARE CENTER AT NYH-CMC      308  2 10    150        500.00
*HOMES FOR THE HOMELESS,INC       309  2 10    150     10,000.00
*MARCH OF DIMES                   310  2 10    150      5,000.00
*BETTER WORLD SOCEITY             311  2 10    150      5,000.00
*THE HEBREW HOME FOR THE AGED     312  2 10    150      5,000.00
*FUND FOR AGING SERVICES          313  2 10    150        500.00
*FUND FOR AGING SERVICES          314  2 11    150     10,000.00
*THE BUCKLEY SCHOOL               315  2 11    150      5,000.00
*THE BUCKLEY SCHOOL               316  2 11    150     25,000.00
*THE IRVINGTON INSTITUTE          317  2 11    150        500.00
*BARBARA SINATRA CHILDRENS CTR    318  2 11    150      5,000.00
*GODS LOVE WE DELIVER             319  2 11    150      1,000.00
*FOUND. FOR ILEITIS & COLITIS     321  2 11    150      1,000.00
*GREENWICH POLICE DEPT            322  2 11    150      1,000.00
*AMFAR                            323  2 11    150      2,000.00
*UNITED CEREBRAL PALSEY           324  2 11    150      5,000.00
*FIGHT FOR SIGHT                  325  2 11    150      1,200.00
```

A list of some of the contributions made by the Donald J. Trump Foundation in 1988. As highlighted here, the donations to his son's school are significantly more than those to AIDS research.

society galas, his high school, his college, a foundation for indigent real estate brokers. The School of American Ballet, where Ivanka Trump studied from 1989 to 1991, got $16,750.

A private school that educated Trump's son Eric got $40,000 — more than the homeless and AIDS contributions combined.

'WANT TO KEEP THEM PRIVATE'

By the early 2000s, Trump had recovered from his financial troubles, returning to the public eye as a different kind of mogul. More than ever, Trump himself was the product: He was selling his name on products from TV shows to steaks to high-rise condominiums throughout the country.

Again, Trump needed an explanation for why he needed the money.

"You're getting paid over a million for your show," radio host Howard Stern said to Trump in 2004, when Trump was first hosting "The Apprentice."

"Oh, a lot more than that," Trump said.

"You're getting paid over $2 1/2 million!" Stern said.

"Yeah, I don't do it for that," Trump said. "I'm giving the money to charity." He named AIDS research and the Police Athletic League. That year, Trump's foundation appears to have given $1,000 to AIDS research and $106,000 to the Police Athletic League.

As the years passed, Trump's promises tended to become less and less specific. He often said he was giving to "charity" without specifying a group or a broader cause.

In at least one case, Trump didn't say anything about donating the proceeds until two years after the transaction occurred.

When Libyan strongman Moammar Gaddafi visited New York in 2009, Trump rented him space for a huge tent at an estate Trump owns north of the city. He said nothing about giving the proceeds to charity.

Two years later, Trump told a television interviewer, "I said when I did it, 'I'm going to take Gaddafi's money ... and I'm going to give the money to charity,' and that's exactly what I did."

BuzzFeed recently estimated Trump's take from Gaddafi at $150,000. If Trump did donate the money, there is no public trace of it; he donated nothing that year to his own foundation. And this spring, Trump seemed to have forgotten his vow to give the money to charity: "I made a lot of money with Gaddafi, if you remember," he told CBS.

In 2008, Trump said that he would send proceeds from

sales of Trump Super Premium Vodka to the Walter Reed Society, which helps wounded military personnel. John Pierce, one of the group's board members, recalls receiving "a few hundred dollars."

In 2011, Trump pledged to forgo his appearance fee for a televised "roast." The Trump Foundation's tax filings show a $400,000 donation from Comedy Central instead. In recent years, the Trump Foundation's coffers have been filled by other donors, not Trump.

One of the clearest cases of Trump not making good on a promise to give to charity is Trump University, the real estate seminar business that has spawned lawsuits in New York and California alleging widespread fraud.

Trump made at least $5 million from Trump University, according to the New York state attorney general. But Trump's attorneys say that none of it went to charity, because it was used for legal fees.

Trump's representatives have repeatedly said that there have been many charitable donations from Trump in recent years but that he has purposely kept them under wraps.

"We want to keep them private. We want to keep them quiet," Allen Weisselberg, the chief financial officer of Trump's business, told The Post earlier this year. "He doesn't want other charities to see it. Then it becomes like a feeding frenzy."

This year, The Post got the same response when it probed a separate claim that Trump had made about his charitable giving. At the launch of his campaign, Trump said that he had given away $102 million in the past five years. That figure turned out to comprise mostly land-use agreements and free rounds of golf given away at Trump's courses.

Trump's campaign said that none of the $102 million it had counted was actually a cash gift from Trump's pocket. Such gifts existed, Trump's staff said. But they were private.

If so, those gifts are remarkably difficult to find.

Of the 188 charities reviewed by The Post — a list compiled with the help of DonorSearch, a private firm with a database of 101 million individual gifts — 44 charities declined to comment. Forty-eight, including the Eric Trump Foundation, did not respond to The Post's inquiries.

An additional 85 charities had no record of receiving a personal donation from Trump.

That left 11 that acknowledged receiving the kind of personal donation that Trump claims to be giving all the time.

The most recent of those was the gift to the Police Athletic League in 2009.

David Fahrenthold ✓
@Fahrenthold

Following ⌄

Got something else fun on @realDonaldTrump coming in an hour or two.

RETWEETS
26

LIKES
84

11:56 AM - 18 Aug 2016

↩ 10   ⇄ 26   ♥ 84

Trump promised personal gifts on 'Celebrity Apprentice.' Here's who really paid.

By David A. Fahrenthold and Alice Crites
August 19, 2016

WASHINGTON — THE TIME HAD COME TO FIRE KHLOÉ Kardashian. But first, Donald Trump had a question.

"What's your charity?" Trump asked.

They were filming "The Celebrity Apprentice," the reality-TV show where Trump schooled the faded and the semi-famous in the arts of advertising, salesmanship and workplace infighting. Most weeks, one winner got prize money for charity. One loser got fired.

Kardashian told Trump that she was playing for the Brent Shapiro Foundation, which helps teens stay away from alcohol and drugs.

Trump had a pleasant surprise. Although Kardashian could not win any more prize money, he would give her cause a special, personal donation. Not the show's money. His own money.

"I'm going to give $20,000 to your charity," Trump said, according to a transcript of that show.

He didn't.

After the show aired in 2009, Kardashian's charity did receive $20,000. But it wasn't from Trump. Instead, the check came from a TV production company, the same one that paid out the show's official prizes.

The same thing happened numerous times on "The Celebrity Apprentice." To console a fired or disappointed celebrity, Trump would promise a personal gift.

On-air, Trump seemed to be explicit that this wasn't TV fakery: The money he was giving was his own. "Out of my wallet," Trump said in one case. "Out of my own account," he said in another.

But, when the cameras were off, the payments came from other people's money.

In some cases, as with Kardashian, Trump's "personal" promise was paid off by a production company. Other times, it was paid off by a nonprofit that Trump controls, whose coffers are largely filled with other donors' money.

The Washington Post tracked all the "personal" gifts that Trump promised on the show — during 83 episodes and seven seasons — but could not confirm a single case in which Trump actually sent a gift from his own pocket.

Trump did not respond to repeated requests for comment.

For Trump, "The Apprentice" — and later, "The Celebrity Apprentice" — helped reestablish him as a

Donald Trump casting for "The Apprentice" in 2004. (Ric Francis/ Associated Press)

national figure, after his fall into debt and corporate bank-ruptcies in the 1990s.

On-screen, Trump was a wise, tough businessman. And, at times, a kindhearted philanthropist — willing to give away thousands on a whim.

In one instance, Trump's sudden flourish of generosity was enough to move an insult comedian to tears.

"I'm gonna give $10,000 to it, okay?" Trump said, offering a personal gift to singer Aubrey O'Day after O'Day's team lost that week's task. Then Trump noticed another contestant, Lisa Lampanelli — a comedian known as "The Queen of Mean. "Are you crying now? Lisa, what's going on here?"

"I thought that was really nice," Lampanelli said, her voice breaking. "I mean, it takes you 30 seconds to make that amount, so thank you. You're a rich man, and we appreciate it."

The Post examined Trump's on-air promises as part of its ongoing search for evidence that the Republican presidential nominee gives millions to charity out of his own pocket — as he claims. Trump has declined to release his tax returns, which would make his charitable donations clear.

NBC, which broadcast his show, declined to release the episodes for review, saying it did not own the footage. Instead, The Post relied on TV transcription services, online recaps of the show, YouTube clips and public tax records.

In all, The Post found 21 separate instances where Trump had pledged money to a celebrity's cause. Together, those pledges totaled $464,000. The Post then contacted the individual charities to find out who paid off Trump's promises.

In one case, the answer was: nobody at all.

In two other cases, it was not possible to determine what happened. One charity said that somebody had paid off Trump's promise but declined to say who. Leaders of another charity — baseball star Darryl Strawberry's foundation, to which Trump had promised $25,000 — did not respond to multiple calls or emails from The Post.

In the other 18 cases, the answer was the same — on-air, Trump promising a gift of his own money; off-air, that gift coming from someone else.

"I think you're so incredible that — personally, out of my own account — I'm going to give you $50,000 for St. Jude's," Trump told mixed martial arts star Tito Ortiz in 2008.

This was the first personal promise The Post found, from the show's first season.

Ortiz, at the time, was being fired. His team had come

up short in a contest to design advertising for yogurt-based body wash. To soften the blow, Trump promised the gift to Ortiz's charity, St. Jude Children's Research Hospital in Memphis.

Tax records show that the hospital was sent $50,000 from a nonprofit, the Donald J. Trump Foundation.

That sounds like it was Trump's money.

But, for the most part, it wasn't.

Trump had founded the nonprofit group in the late 1980s — and, in its early years, Trump was its only donor. But that had changed in the mid-2000s. Trump let the foundation's assets dwindle to $4,238 at the beginning of 2007. After that, its coffers were filled using donations from others, most notably pro wrestling magnates Vince and Linda McMahon.

In 2007 and 2008 combined, Trump gave $65,000 to his own foundation, or about 1 percent of its incoming money.

When he described his gift to Ortiz on-air in 2008, it was personal, "from my own account."

"Thank you very much," Ortiz said.

"Get out of here," Trump said.

In the next few seasons, such personal promises from Trump were relatively rare. The Post found six such pledges in the show's first four seasons combined.

And in at least two of those cases, the payment didn't come from Trump — or his foundation, which he had used to pay Ortiz's charity.

"What's your charity, Jose?" Trump asked baseball slugger Jose Canseco in an episode in 2011. Canseco was leaving the show voluntarily because his father had become ill. As with Kardashian, Trump said he would soften

Actor Gary Busey attends "The Celebrity Apprentice" Season 4 finale in 2011. (Neilson Barnard/Getty Images)

the blow with a gift. Canseco's charity was the Baseball Assistance Team, which provides confidential aid to minor leaguers, umpires, retired players and others connected to the sport.

"All right, I'm gonna give $25,000," Trump said. "Say hello to your father."

As with Kardashian, that money came from Reilly Worldwide. Trump gave nothing.

The Post sent a query to Canseco: Did he think any differently about Trump after he learned that a third party paid off Trump's promise?

No comment. "He said he's only doing paying jobs. I'm sorry," Canseco's publicist wrote.

In 2012, Trump became more generous on the air.

That year, he promised six $10,000 donations in a single

episode. In another episode, he gave contestant O'Day's charity $10,000 — the gift that moved Lampanelli to tears.

It was all Trump Foundation money.

In 2013, the gifts continued. In one episode that year, Trump handed out $20,000 each to the charities of basketball star Dennis Rodman, singer La Toya Jackson and actor Gary Busey.

"Remember, Donald Trump is a very nice person, okay?" he told them.

By then, a personal gift from Trump was no longer a rare thing. In fact, contestants had come to expect these gifts — and even to demand them, when Trump didn't offer money on his own.

"Give her some money. She didn't win nothin'," country singer Trace Adkins told Trump in one episode as the billionaire was firing former Playboy Playmate Brande Roderick.

"Okay, I'm going to give you $20,000, okay? All right?" Trump told Roderick.

"Thank you, Mr. Trump," said Adkins, the man who sang "Honky Tonk Badonkadonk." "That was cool."

All of that was the Trump Foundation's money.

In fact, The Post's search found that all of Trump's promises from the show's last three seasons were paid off by the Trump Foundation, save one. That was the biggest one. In 2013, Trump promised $100,000 to the American Diabetes Association, the charity of hip-hop artist Lil Jon. He said that the gift was in honor of Lil Jon's mother, who had recently died.

In that case, a production company paid.

The Post reached out to Trump, NBC and Mark

From left, Penn Jillette, Lil Jon and Trace Adkins attend an "All Star Celebrity Apprentice" event at Trump Tower in 2013. (Slaven Vlasic/ Getty Images)

Burnett — the show's producer — to ask whether there was any way that these production-company checks could actually be considered gifts from Trump himself. Had they, perhaps, been deducted from Trump's fees for the show?

Trump and Burnett did not respond. NBC declined to comment.

After The Post's close look at Trump's promises on the show, a mystery remained: What happened in 2012 to make Trump so much more generous on the air?

In the tax records of the Trump Foundation — which Trump used to pay off most of those new promises — there is no record of a donation from Trump himself in 2012.

In fact, there is no record of any gift from Trump's pocket to the Trump Foundation in any year since 2008.

(In 2011, Comedy Central donated Trump's $400,000 appearance fee for a televised roast.)

But, in 2012, the Trump Foundation's records show a large gift from NBC, the network that aired the show. That was more than enough to cover all the foundation's gifts to "Celebrity Apprentice" contestants' charities, both before 2012 and since.

For NBC, Trump's "personal" donations made for better TV. They added will-he-or-won't-he drama to the show's boardroom scenes, gave uplifting notes to the "firings" and burnished the reputation of Trump, the show's star.

Did NBC give Trump's foundation money, so that Trump could appear to be more generous on-camera?

An NBC spokeswoman declined to comment.

Rosalind S. Helderman contributed to this report.

David Fahrenthold ✓
@Fahrenthold

Closing in on a milestone: almost 300 charities contacted, in my search for @realdonaldtrump's missing donations.

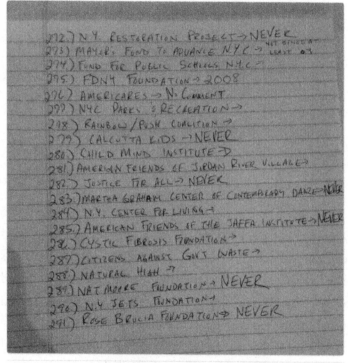

272.) N.Y. RESTORATION PROJECT → NEVER
273.) MAYOR'S FUND TO ADVANCE N.Y.C → NOT SINCE AT LEAST 03
274.) FUND FOR PUBLIC SCHOOLS N.Y.C →
275.) FDNY FOUNDATION → 2008
276.) AMERICARES → N. COMMENT
277.) NYC PARKS & RECREATION →
278.) RAINBOW/PUSH COALITION →
279.) CALCUTTA KIDS → NEVER
280.) CHILD MIND INSTITUTE →
281.) AMERICAN FRIENDS OF JORDAN RIVER VILLAGE →
282.) JUSTICE FOR ALL → NEVER
283.) MARTHA GRAHAM CENTER OF CONTEMPORARY DANCE → NEVER
284.) N.Y. CENTER FOR LIVING →
285.) AMERICAN FRIENDS OF THE JAFFA INSTITUTE → NEVER
286.) CYSTIC FIBROSIS FOUNDATION →
287.) CITIZENS AGAINST GOVT WASTE →
288.) NATURAL HIGH →
289.) NAT MOORE FOUNDATION → NEVER
290.) N.Y. JETS FOUNDATION →
291.) ROSE BRUCIA FOUNDATION → NEVER

RETWEETS	LIKES
272	295

10:08 AM - 31 Aug 2016

↩ 14   ♺ 272   ♥ 295

Trump pays IRS a penalty for his foundation violating rules with gift to aid Florida attorney general

By David A. Fahrenthold

Sept. 1, 2016

DONALD TRUMP PAID THE IRS A $2,500 PENALTY THIS year, an official at Trump's company said, after it was revealed that Trump's charitable foundation had violated tax laws by giving a political contribution to a campaign group connected to Florida's attorney general.

The improper donation, a $25,000 gift from the Donald J. Trump Foundation, was made in 2013. At the time, Attorney General Pam Bondi was considering whether to investigate fraud allegations against Trump University. She decided not to pursue the case.

Earlier this year, The Washington Post and a liberal watchdog group raised new questions about the three-year-

Donald Trump is greeted by Florida Attorney General Pam Bondi at a March 14 campaign event in Tampa. (Gerald Herbert/Associated Press)

old gift. The watchdog group, Citizens for Responsibility and Ethics in Washington, filed a complaint with the IRS — noting that, as a registered nonprofit, the Trump Foundation was not allowed to make political donations.

The Post reported another error, which had the effect of obscuring the political gift from the IRS.

In that year's tax filings, The Post reported, the Trump Foundation did not notify the IRS of this political donation. Instead, Trump's foundation listed a donation — also for $25,000 — to a Kansas charity with a name similar to that of Bondi's political group. In fact, Trump's foundation had not given the Kansas group any money.

The prohibited gift was, in effect, replaced with an innocent-sounding but nonexistent donation.

Trump's business said it was unaware of any of these

mistakes until March, when it heard from the watchdog group and The Post.

On Thursday, Jeffrey McConney — senior vice president and controller at the Trump Organization — said that after being notified, Trump filed paperwork informing the IRS of the political gift and paid an excise tax equal to 10 percent of its value.

McConney said that Trump had also personally reimbursed the Trump Foundation for $25,000, covering the full value of the improper gift. McConney blamed a series of mistakes, all of them unintentional. McConney said there had been no attempt to deceive.

"It was just an honest mistake," McConney said. He added: "It wasn't done intentionally to hide a political donation, it was just an error."

McConney said that he believed Trump had now done everything necessary to rectify the error. "We've done what [we] were instructed to do," he said.

Trump started the Donald J. Trump Foundation in the late 1980s, to give away proceeds from his book, "The Art of the Deal." He remains the foundation's president, but — in recent years — Trump has stopped putting his own money into its coffers. Tax records show no gifts from Trump himself to the foundation since 2008; it has instead received donations from a smattering of Trump's friends and business associates.

The Trump Foundation has no paid staff and relatively little money for a superwealthy man's personal charity: At the end of 2014, it had $1.3 million in the bank. The foundation's giving is small and scattershot, with its gifts often sent to people whom Trump knows, or charities that hold their galas at his properties in New York and Florida.

In this case, Trump staffers said that a series of unusual — and unrelated — errors by people working for Trump had led to both the improper donation and to the omission of that donation from the foundation's tax filings.

The sequence began when Bondi herself solicited a donation from Trump. That solicitation was reported this year by the Associated Press. That request came as Bondi was considering allegations that Trump University — a real estate seminar business — had defrauded customers in Florida.

Trump decided to give to the group connected to Bondi, called "And Justice for All."

Then, a request for a check was sent to an accounts-payable clerk at Trump's headquarters. This clerk was empowered to cut checks from both Trump's personal account and from the Trump Foundation.

In most cases, political contributions were paid out of Trump's own account. But, in this case, that didn't happen.

In March, Trump's chief financial officer told The Post that a mistake occurred when an accounting clerk — following office protocol — looked in a book that contained a list of all official charities. The clerk's standing order from Trump was that, if the payee was listed in this book of charities, the check should be paid from the Trump Foundation, not from Trump's own account.

The clerk found a group called "And Justice for All" listed in the book.

The clerk cut the check from the Trump Foundation.

But that was wrong.

Trump's chief financial officer, Allen Weisselberg, told The Post that the charity in the book was actually from Utah, and unconnected to Bondi. If the clerk had known that the check was meant for a political group, Weisselberg said, "we would have taken it out of [Trump's] own personal account."

After that, a check from the foundation went out. It did not go to Utah but to Bondi's group in Florida, and was deposited.

Then, when the Trump Foundation sent in its tax filings that year, it compounded the original error by leaving out any mention of a political gift. When the IRS form asked if the Trump Foundation had spent money for political purposes that year, the foundation wrote "No."

11	Enter the amount of line 10 to be Credited to 2014 estimated tax ▸	381 Refunded	▸	11			0

Part VII-A   Statements Regarding Activities

			Yes	No
1a	During the tax year, did the foundation attempt to influence any national, state, or local legislation or did it participate or intervene in any political campaign? **1a**			No
b	Did it spend more than $100 during the year (either directly or indirectly) for political purposes (see page 19 of the instructions for definition)? **1b**			No

A section of the Trump Foundation's 2013 tax filing, in which the foundation said it had not engaged in political activity. In fact, it had sent a check to a political group in Florida, in violation of IRS rules.

Then, the Trump Foundation told the IRS about a gift that did not exist.

The foundation told the IRS that it had given $25,000 to a third group, a charity in Kansas with a similar name, "Justice for All." In fact, the Trump Foundation had not actually sent the Kansas group any money.

This new, incorrect listing had the effect of camouflaging the prohibited gift. Trump's CFO said that the listing

NEW YORK, NY 10018				
JULIE'S JUNGLE 5 LIME KILN RD HOPEWELL JUNCTION, NY 12533			GENERAL	12,500
JUSTICE FOR ALL 113 N MARTINSON ST WICHITA, KS 67203			GENERAL	25,000
LEADERS IN FURTHERING EDUCATION 1720S OCEAN BLVD			GENERAL	6,000

An excerpt from the 2013 tax filings of the Donald J. Trump Foundation. The $25,000 gift to "Justice for All" did not exist. It took the place of a real $25,000 gift that had violated IRS rules, because it went to a campaign group in Florida. The name of the group that got the prohibited gift: "And Justice for All."

of the Kansas group was another mistake, made by the foundation's accountants.

The Post asked McConney, the Trump Organization controller, for a copy of the IRS form that Trump had filed along with his $2,500 penalty tax. McConney said he would check to see if it could be released.

The IRS declined to comment about the situation.

But on Thursday, the liberal watchdog group said that the Trump Foundation needs to do more that it has. Under IRS rules, it appears that the Trump Foundation must seek to get the money back from the political group.

Although Trump has apparently reimbursed the foundation, "that's not the same," said Jordan Libowitz, of Citizens for Responsibility and Ethics in Washington. "It's about getting the money back from the organization that wasn't allowed to have it in the first place."

So far, that hasn't happened.

In fact, the treasurer of Bondi's political group said that she had actually tried to send the money back, without success.

"I wrote a check, sent it via FedEx. I received a call from the Trump Foundation, saying that they had declined to accept the refund," said Nancy Watkins in an interview with The Post. She said this had happened in the spring, after she learned that the Trump Foundation was not allowed to make political gifts.

Watkins said she was told, "Mr. Trump had reimbursed the foundation with a personal check. And that was the end of it."

David Fahrenthold ✔
@Fahrenthold

Stand by for a new look at @realdonaldtrump's charity, and a new challenge for readers. There's something out there I need you all to locate

RETWEETS	LIKES	
95	201	

3:40 PM - 10 Sep 2016

↩ 31   ⟲ 95   ♥ 201

How Donald Trump retooled his charity to spend other people's money

By David A. Fahrenthold
Sept. 10, 2016

Donald Trump was in a tuxedo, standing next to his award: a statue of a palm tree, as tall as a toddler. It was 2010, and Trump was being honored by a charity — the Palm Beach Police Foundation — for his "selfless support" of its cause.

His support did not include any of his own money.

Instead, Trump had found a way to give away somebody else's money and claim the credit for himself.

Trump had earlier gone to a charity in New Jersey — the Charles Evans Foundation, named for a deceased businessman — and asked for a donation. Trump said he was raising money for the Palm Beach Police Foundation.

The Evans Foundation said yes. In 2009 and 2010, it gave a total of $150,000 to the Donald J. Trump

Donations to the Donald J. Trump Foundation

● TRUMP ○ OTHER DONORS

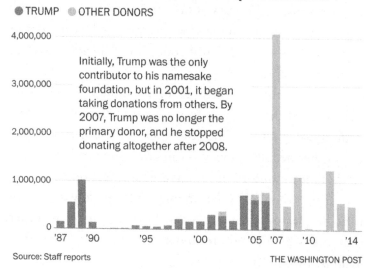

Initially, Trump was the only contributor to his namesake foundation, but in 2001, it began taking donations from others. By 2007, Trump was no longer the primary donor, and he stopped donating altogether after 2008.

Source: Staff reports

THE WASHINGTON POST

Foundation, a small charity that the Republican presidential nominee founded in 1987.

Then, Trump's foundation turned around and made donations to the police group in South Florida. In those years, the Trump Foundation's gifts totaled $150,000.

Trump had effectively turned the Evans Foundation's gifts into his own gifts, without adding any money of his own.

On the night that he won the Palm Tree Award for his philanthropy, Trump may have actually made money. The gala was held at his Mar-a-Lago Club in Palm Beach, and the police foundation paid to rent the room. It's unclear how much was paid in 2010, but the police foundation reported in its tax filings that it rented Mar-a-Lago in 2014 for $276,463.

The Donald J. Trump Foundation is not like other

charities. An investigation of the foundation — including examinations of 17 years of tax filings and interviews with more than 200 individuals or groups listed as donors or beneficiaries — found that it collects and spends money in a very unusual manner.

For one thing, nearly all of its money comes from people other than Trump. In tax records, the last gift from Trump was in 2008. Since then, all of the donations have been other people's money — an arrangement that experts say is almost unheard of for a family foundation.

Trump then takes that money and generally does with it as he pleases. In many cases, he passes it on to other charities, which often are under the impression that it is Trump's own money.

In two cases, he has used money from his charity to buy himself a gift. In one of those cases — not previously reported — Trump spent $20,000 of money earmarked for charitable purposes to buy a six-foot-tall painting of himself.

Money from the Trump Foundation has also been used for political purposes, which is against the law. The Washington Post reported this month that Trump paid a penalty this year to the Internal Revenue Service for a 2013 donation in which the foundation gave $25,000 to a campaign group affiliated with Florida Attorney General Pamela Bondi (R).

Trump's foundation appears to have repeatedly broken IRS rules, which require nonprofit groups to file accurate paperwork. In five cases, the Trump Foundation told the IRS that it had given a gift to a charity whose leaders told The Post that they had never received it. In two other cases, companies listed as donors to the Trump Foundation told The Post that those listings were incorrect.

Last week, The Post submitted a detailed list of questions about the Trump Foundation to Trump's campaign. Officials with the campaign declined to comment.

Trump and his Democratic opponent, Hillary Clinton, have both been criticized during their campaigns for activities related to their foundations.

Critics have charged that the giant Bill, Hillary and Chelsea Clinton Foundation, which employs more than 2,000 people and spends about a quarter of a billion dollars a year, has served as a way for businesses and powerful figures across the world to curry favor with one of America's most powerful families. The Clinton Foundation has also been credited by supporters and critics alike for its charitable efforts.

Trump has claimed that he gives generously to charity from his own pocket: "I don't have to give you records," he told The Post earlier this year, "but I've given millions away." Efforts to verify those gifts have not succeeded, and Trump has refused to release his tax returns, which would show his charitable giving.

That leaves the Trump Foundation as the best window into the GOP nominee's philanthropy.

In the past several days, questions about Trump's foundation have focused on the gift to Bondi's group in 2013. At the time the money arrived, Bondi's office was considering whether to launch an investigation into allegations of fraud by Trump University — accusations that Trump denies.

The investigation never started. Aides to Bondi and Trump say the gift and the case were unrelated. But

Democrats have seized on what they see as a clear example of political influence improperly funded by Trump's charity.

"The foundation was being used basically to promote a moneymaking fraudulent venture of Donald Trump's. That's not what charities are supposed to do," Virginia Sen. Tim Kaine, Clinton's running mate, said Friday. "I hope there's a significant effort to get to the bottom of it and find out whether this is the end."

A THREADBARE OPERATION

Trump started his foundation in 1987 with a narrow purpose: to give away some of the proceeds from his book "The Art of the Deal."

Nearly three decades later, the Trump Foundation is still a threadbare, skeletal operation.

The most money it has ever reported having was $3.2 million at the end of 2009. At last count, that total had shrunk to $1.3 million. By comparison, Oprah Winfrey — who is worth $1.5 billion less than Trump, according to a Forbes magazine estimate — has a foundation with $242 million in the bank. At the end of 2014, the Clinton Foundation had $440 million in assets.

In a few cases, Trump seemed to solicit donations only to immediately give them away. But his foundation has also received a handful of bigger donations — including $5 million from professional-wrestling executives Vince and Linda McMahon — that Trump handed out a little at a time.

The foundation has no paid staffers. It has an unpaid

board consisting of four Trumps — Donald, Ivanka, Eric and Donald Jr. — and one Trump Organization employee.

In 2014, at last report, each said they worked a half-hour a week.

The Trump Foundation still gives out small, scattered gifts — which seem driven by the demands of Trump's businesses and social life, rather than by a desire to support charitable causes.

The foundation makes a few dozen donations a year, usually in amounts from $1,000 to $50,000. It gives to charities that rent Trump's ballrooms. It gives to charities whose leaders buttonholed Trump on the golf course (and then try, in vain, to get him to offer a repeat donation the next year).

It even gives in situations in which Trump publicly put himself on the hook for a donation — as when he promised a gift "out of my wallet" on NBC's "The Celebrity Apprentice." The Trump Foundation paid off most of those on-air promises. A TV production company paid others. The Post could find no instance in which a celebrity's charity got a gift from Trump's own wallet.

Another time, Trump went on TV's "Extra" for a contest called "Trump pays your bills!"

A professional spray-tanner won. The Trump Foundation paid her bills.

A RARITY AMONG CHARITIES

About 10 years ago, the Trump Foundation underwent a

major change — although it was invisible to those who received its gifts.

The checks still had Trump's name on them.

Behind the scenes, he was transforming the foundation from a standard-issue rich person's philanthropy into a charity that allowed a rich man to be philanthropic for free.

Experts on charity said they had rarely seen anything like it.

"Our common understanding of charity is you give something of yourself to help somebody else. It's not something that you raise money from one side to spend it on the other," said Leslie Lenkowsky, the former head of the Corporation for National and Community Service, and a professor studying philanthropy at Indiana University.

By that definition, was Trump engaging in charity?

No, Lenkowsky said.

"It's a deal," he said, an arrangement worked out for maximum benefit at minimum sacrifice.

In the Trump Foundation's early days, between 1987 and 2006, Trump actually was its primary donor. Over that span, Trump gave his own foundation a total of $5.4 million. But he was giving it away as fast as he put it in, and by the start of 2007, the foundation's assets had dropped to $4,238.

Then, Trump made a change.

First, he stopped giving his own money.

His contribution shrank to $35,000 in 2007.

Then to $30,000 in 2008.

Then to $0.

At the same time, Trump's foundation began to fill with money from other people.

But in many other cases, his biggest donors have not wanted to say why they gave their own money, when Trump was giving none of his.

"I don't have time for this. Thank you," said Richard Ebers, a ticket broker in New York City who has given the Trump Foundation $1.9 million since 2011.

"No. No. No. I'm not going to comment on anything. I'm not answering any of your questions," said John Stark, the chief executive of a carpet company that has donated $64,000 over the years.

Vince and Linda McMahon declined to comment.

So did NBCUniversal, which donated $500,000 in 2012. Its gift more than covered the "personal" donations that Trump offered at dramatic moments on "The Celebrity Apprentice" — then paid for out of the Trump Foundation.

Trump's donations to the Palm Beach Police Foundation offered a stark example of Trump turning somebody else's gift into his own charity.

Tax experts said they had rarely heard of anything like what Trump had done, converting another donor's gift into his own.

"I question whether it's ethical. It's certainly misleading. But I think it's legal, because you would think that the other foundation that's ... being taken advantage of would look out for their own interests," said Rosemary E. Fei, an attorney in San Francisco who has advised hundreds of small foundations. "That's their decision to let him do that."

After three years, the Charles Evans Foundation stopped using Trump as a middleman.

"We realized we don't need to do it through a pass-through," said Bonnie Pfeifer Evans, the widow of Charles Evans and a trustee of the now-defunct foundation.

In 2012, the Charles Evans Foundation stopped giving money to the Trump Foundation.

In 2013, according to tax records, the Trump Foundation stopped giving to the Palm Beach Police Foundation.

The police group, which gave Trump the award, did not know that Trump's money had come from somebody else's pocket. It could not explain why he gave in some years but not others — or why he gave in the amounts he did.

"He's the unpredictable guy, right?" said John F. Scarpa, the Palm Beach Police Foundation's president, before The Post informed him about how Trump got the money. He said Trump's giving wasn't the only reason he got the award. He also could be counted on to draw a crowd to the group's annual event. The amount paid to Trump's club was first reported by BuzzFeed.

The police group still holds its galas at Mar-a-Lago.

ACTS OF 'SELF-DEALING'

At the same time that it began to rely on other people's money, the Trump Foundation sometimes appeared to flout IRS rules by purchasing things that seemed to benefit only Trump.

In 2007, for instance, Trump and his wife, Melania, attended a benefit for a children's charity held at Mar-a-Lago. The night's entertainment was Michael Israel, who bills himself as "the original speed painter." His frenetic act involved painting giant portraits in five to seven minutes — then auctioning off the art he'd just created.

He painted Trump.

Melania Trump bid $10,000.

Nobody tried to outbid her.

"The auctioneer was just pretty bold, so he said, 'You know what just happened: When you started bidding, nobody's going to bid against you, and I think it's only fair that you double the bid,'" Israel said in an interview last week.

Melania Trump increased her bid to $20,000.

"I understand it went to one of his golf courses," Israel said of the painting.

The Trump Foundation paid the $20,000, according to the charity that held the benefit.

Something similar happened in 2012, when Trump himself won an auction for a football helmet autographed by football player Tim Tebow, then a quarterback with the Denver Broncos.

The winning bid was $12,000. As The Post reported in July, the Trump Foundation paid.

IRS rules generally prohibit acts of "self-dealing," in which a charity's leaders use the nonprofit group's money to buy things for themselves.

In both years, IRS forms asked whether the foundation had broken those rules: Had it "furnish[ed] goods, services or facilities" to Trump or another of its officers?

In both years, the Trump Foundation checked "no."

Tax experts said Trump could have avoided violating the self-dealing rules if he gave the helmet and the painting to other charities instead of keeping them. Trump's staffers have not said where the two items are now.

The IRS penalties for acts of "self-dealing" can include penalty taxes, both on charities and on their leaders as individuals.

In other cases, the Trump Foundation's tax filings appeared to include listings that were incorrect.

The most prominent example is the improper political donation to the group affiliated with Bondi, the Florida attorney general, in 2013. In that case, Trump's staffers said a series of errors resulted in the payment being made — and then hidden from the IRS.

First, Trump officials said, when the request came down to cut a check to the Bondi group, a Trump Organization clerk followed internal protocol and consulted a book with the names of known charities.

The name of the pro-Bondi group is "And Justice for All." Trump's staffer saw that name in the book, and — mistakenly — cut the check from the Trump Foundation. The group in the book was an entirely different charity in Utah, unrelated to Bondi's group in Florida.

Somehow, the money got to Florida anyway.

Then, Trump's staffers said, the foundation's accounting firm made another mistake: It told the IRS that the $25,000 had gone to a third charity, based in Kansas, called Justice for All. In reality, the Kansas group got no money.

"That was just a complete mess-up on names. Anything that could go wrong did go wrong," Jeffrey McConney, the Trump Organization's controller, told The Post last week. After The Post pointed out these errors in the spring, Trump paid a $2,500 penalty tax.

DONATIONS NOT RECEIVED

In four other cases, The Post found charities that said they never received donations that the Trump Foundation said it gave them.

The amounts were small: $10,000 in 2008, $5,000 in 2010, $10,000 in 2012. Most of the charities had no idea that Trump had said he had given them money.

One did.

This January, the phone rang at a tiny charity in White River Junction, Vt., called Friends of Veterans. This was just after Trump had held a televised fundraiser for veterans in Iowa, raising more than $5 million.

The man on the phone was a Trump staffer who was selecting charities that would receive the newly raised money. He said the Vermont group was already on Trump's list, because the Trump Foundation had given it $1,000 in 2013.

"I don't remember a donation from the Trump Foundation," said Larry Daigle, the group's president, who was a helicopter gunner with the Army during the Vietnam War. "The guy seemed pretty surprised about this."

The man went away from the phone. He came back. Was Daigle sure? He was.

The man thanked him. He hung up. Daigle waited — hopes raised — for the Trump people to call back.

"Oh, my God, do you know how many homeless veterans I could help?" Daigle told The Post this spring, while he was waiting.

Trump gave away the rest of the veterans money in late May.

Daigle's group got none of it.

In two other cases, the Trump Foundation reported to the IRS that it had received donations from two companies that have denied making such gifts. In 2013, for instance, the Trump Foundation said it had received a $100,000 donation from the Clancy Law Firm, whose offices are in a Trump-owned building on Wall Street.

"That's incorrect," said Donna Clancy, the firm's founder, when The Post called. "I'm not answering any questions."

She hung up and did not respond to requests for comment afterward.

"All of these things show that the [Trump] foundation is run in a less-than-ideal manner. But that's not at all unusual for small, private foundations, especially those run by a family," said Brett Kappel, a Washington attorney who advises tax-exempt organizations. "Usually, you have an accounting firm that has access to the bank statements, and they're the ones who find these errors and correct them."

The Trump Foundation's accountants are at WeiserMazars, a New York-based firm. The Post sent them a detailed list of questions, asking them to explain these possible errors.

The firm declined to comment.

Rosalind S. Helderman contributed to this report.

David Fahrenthold ✓
@Fahrenthold

Found it.

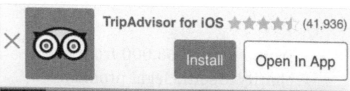

TripAdvisor for iOS ★★★★✰ (41,936)

×  Install | Open In App

RETWEETS **1,539**   LIKES **4,246**

6:07 PM - 20 Sep 2016

↩ 325   ⟲ 1.5K   ♥ 4.2K

Trump used $258,000 from his charity to settle legal problems

By David A. Fahrenthold
Sept. 20, 2016

DONALD TRUMP SPENT MORE THAN A QUARTER-MILLION dollars from his charitable foundation to settle lawsuits that involved the billionaire's for-profit businesses, according to interviews and a review of legal documents.

Those cases, which together used $258,000 from Trump's charity, were among four newly documented expenditures in which Trump may have violated laws against "self-dealing" — which prohibit nonprofit leaders from using charity money to benefit themselves or their businesses.

In one case, from 2007, Trump's Mar-a-Lago Club faced $120,000 in unpaid fines from the town of Palm Beach, Fla., resulting from a dispute over the height of a flagpole.

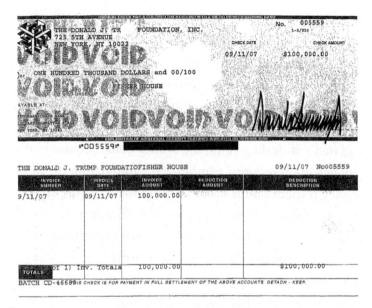

The check to charity from the Trump Foundation.

In a settlement, Palm Beach agreed to waive those fines — if Trump's club made a $100,000 donation to a specific charity for veterans. Instead, Trump sent a check from the Donald J. Trump Foundation, a charity funded almost entirely by other people's money, according to tax records.

In another case, court papers say one of Trump's golf courses in New York agreed to settle a lawsuit by making a donation to the plaintiff's chosen charity. A $158,000 donation was made by the Trump Foundation, according to tax records.

The other expenditures involved smaller amounts. In 2013, Trump used $5,000 from the foundation to buy advertisements touting his chain of hotels in programs for three events organized by a D.C. preservation group. And in 2014, Trump spent $10,000 of the foundation's money on a portrait of himself bought at a charity fundraiser.

Or, rather, another portrait of himself.

Several years earlier, Trump used $20,000 from the Trump Foundation to buy a different, six-foot-tall portrait.

If the Internal Revenue Service were to find that Trump violated self-dealing rules, the agency could require him to pay penalty taxes or to reimburse the foundation for all the money it spent on his behalf. Trump is also facing scrutiny from the New York attorney general's office, which is examining whether the foundation broke state charity laws.

More broadly, these cases also provide new evidence that Trump ran his charity in a way that may have violated U.S. tax law and gone against the moral conventions of philanthropy.

"I represent 700 nonprofits a year, and I've never encountered anything so brazen," said Jeffrey Tenenbaum, who advises charities at the Venable law firm in Washington. After The Washington Post described the details of these Trump Foundation gifts, Tenenbaum described them as "really shocking."

"If he's using other people's money — run through his foundation — to satisfy his personal obligations, then that's about as blatant an example of self-dealing [as] I've seen in awhile," Tenenbaum said.

The Post sent the Trump campaign a detailed list of questions about the four cases but received no response.

The Trump campaign released a statement about this story late Tuesday that said it was "peppered with inaccuracies and omissions," though the statement cited none and the campaign has still not responded to repeated requests for comment.

The New York attorney general's office declined to comment when asked whether its inquiry would cover these new cases of possible self-dealing.

Trump founded his charity in 1987 and for years was its only donor. But in 2006, Trump gave away almost all the money he had donated to the foundation, leaving it with just $4,238 at year's end, according to tax records.

Then, he transformed the Trump Foundation into something rarely seen in the world of philanthropy: a name-branded foundation whose namesake provides none of its money. Trump gave relatively small donations in 2007 and 2008, and afterward, nothing. The foundation's tax records show no donations from Trump since 2009.

Its money has come from other donors, most notably pro-wrestling executives Vince and Linda McMahon, who gave a total of $5 million from 2007 to 2009, tax records show. Trump remains the foundation's president, and he told the IRS in his latest public filings that he works half an hour per week on the charity.

The Post has previously detailed other cases in which Trump used the charity's money in a way that appeared to violate the law.

In 2013, for instance, the foundation gave $25,000 to a political group supporting Florida Attorney General Pam Bondi (R). That gift was made about the same time that Bondi's office was considering whether to investigate fraud allegations against Trump University. It didn't.

Tax laws say nonprofit groups such as the Trump Foundation may not make political gifts. Trump staffers blamed the gift on a clerical error. After The Post reported on the gift to Bondi's group this spring, Trump paid a $2,500 penalty tax and reimbursed the Trump Foundation for the $25,000 donation.

In other instances, it appeared that Trump may have violated rules against self-dealing.

In 2012, for instance, Trump spent $12,000 of the foundation's money to buy a football helmet signed by then-NFL quarterback Tim Tebow.

And in 2007, Trump's wife, Melania, bid $20,000 for the six-foot-tall portrait of Trump, done by a "speed painter" during a charity gala at Mar-a-Lago. Later, Trump paid for the painting with $20,000 from the foundation.

In those cases, tax experts said, Trump was not allowed to simply keep these items and display them in a home or business. They had to be put to a charitable use.

After the settlement, Trump put a slightly smaller flag farther from the road and mounted it on a 70-foot pole as seen in this Nov. 1, 2015, photo. (Rosalind Helderman/The Washington Post)

Trump's campaign has not responded to questions about what became of the helmet or the portrait.

The four new cases of possible self-dealing were discovered in the Trump Foundation's tax filings. While Trump has refused to release his personal tax returns, the foundation's filings are required to be public.

The case involving the flagpole at Trump's oceanfront Mar-a-Lago Club began in 2006, when the club put up a giant American flag on the 80-foot pole. Town rules said flagpoles should be 42 feet high at most. Trump's contention, according to news reports, was: "You don't need a permit to put up the American flag."

The town began to fine Trump, $1,250 a day.

Trump's club sued in federal court, saying that a smaller flag "would fail to appropriately express the magnitude of Donald J. Trump's ... patriotism."

They settled.

The town waived the $120,000 in fines. In September 2007, Trump wrote the town a letter, saying he had done his part as well.

"I have sent a check for $100,000 to Fisher House," he wrote. The town had chosen Fisher House, which runs a network of comfort homes for the families of veterans and military personnel receiving medical treatment, as the recipient of the money. Trump added that, for good measure, "I have sent a check for $25,000" to another charity, the American Veterans Disabled for Life Memorial.

Trump provided the town with copies of the checks, which show that they came from the Trump Foundation.

In Palm Beach, nobody seems to have objected to the

fines assessed on Trump's business being erased by a donation from a charity.

"I don't know that there was any attention paid to that at the time. We just saw two checks signed by Donald J. Trump," said John Randolph, the Palm Beach town attorney. "I'm sure we were satisfied with it."

current size. The Town will waive the Code Enforcement Board fines against Mar-A-Lago and Mr. Trump will contribute $100,000 to charities agreed to between the Parties. Further, the Parties will exchange mutual releases in the manner and form attached hereto as Exhibit "B."

Excerpt from a settlement filed in federal court in 2007.

In the other case in which a Trump Foundation payment seemed to help settle a legal dispute, the trouble began with a hole-in-one.

In 2010, a man named Martin Greenberg hit a hole-in-one on the 13th hole while playing in a charity golf tournament at Trump's course in Westchester County, N.Y.

Greenberg won a $1 million prize. Briefly.

Later, Greenberg was told that he had won nothing. The prize's rules required that the shot had to go 150 yards. But Trump's course had allegedly made the hole too short.

Greenberg sued.

Eventually, court papers show, Trump's golf course signed off on a settlement that required it to make a donation to a group of Greenberg's choosing. Then, on the day that the parties informed the court they had settled their case, a $158,000 donation was sent to the Martin Greenberg Foundation.

That money came from the Trump Foundation, according to the tax filings of both Trump's and Greenberg's foundations.

Greenberg's foundation reported getting nothing that year from Trump personally or from his golf club.

Both Greenberg and Trump have declined to comment.

Several tax experts said that the two cases appeared to be clear examples of self-dealing, as defined by the tax code.

The Trump Foundation had made a donation, it seemed, so that a Trump business did not have to.

Rosemary E. Fei, a lawyer in San Francisco who advises nonprofit groups, said both cases clearly fit the definition of self-dealing.

"Yes, Trump pledged as part of the settlement to make a payment to a charity, and yes, the foundation is writing a check to a charity," Fei said. "But the obligation was Trump's. And you can't have a charitable foundation paying off Trump's personal obligations. That would be classic self-dealing."

In another instance, from 2013, the Trump Foundation made a $5,000 donation to the D.C. Preservation League, according to the group and tax filings. That nonprofit group's support has been helpful for Trump as he has turned the historic Old Post Office Pavilion on Pennsylvania Avenue NW into a luxury hotel.

The Trump Foundation's donation to that group bought a "sponsorship," which included advertising space

The Trump International Hotel in Washington, a renovation of the historic Old Post Office Pavilion, opened Sept. 12. (Marvin Joseph/The Washington Post)

in the programs for three big events that drew Washington's real estate elite. The ads did not mention the foundation or anything related to charity. Instead, they promoted Trump's hotels, with glamorous photos and a phone number to call to make a reservation.

"The foundation wrote a check that essentially bought advertising for Trump hotels?" asked John Edie, the long-time general counsel for the Council on Foundations, when a Post reporter described this arrangement. "That's not charity."

The last of the four newly documented expenditures involves the second painting of Trump, which he bought with charity money.

It happened in 2014, during a gala at Mar-a-Lago that raised money for Unicorn Children's Foundation — a

Donald Trump
by Havi Schanz
#HaviArt

LEFT: A painting by artist Havi Schanz of Donald Trump. (Photo provided by Havi Schanz) RIGHT: Trump with the painting that he bought. (Photo provided by Havi Schanz)

Florida charity that helps children with developmental and learning disorders.

The gala's main event was a concert by Jon Secada. But there was also an auction of paintings by Havi Schanz, a Miami Beach-based artist.

One was of Marilyn Monroe. The other was a four-foot-tall portrait of Trump: a younger-looking, mid-'90s Trump, painted in acrylic on top of an old architectural drawing.

Trump bought it for $10,000.

Afterward, Schanz recalled in an email, "he asked me about the painting. I said, 'I paint souls, and when I had to paint you, I asked your soul to allow me.' He was touched and smiled."

A few days later, the charity said, a check came from the Trump Foundation. Trump himself gave nothing, according to Sharon Alexander, the executive director of the charity.

Trump's staff did not respond to questions about where that second painting is now. Alexander said she had last seen it at Trump's club.

"I'm pretty sure we just left it at Mar-a-Lago," she said, "and his staff took care of it."

The website TripAdvisor provides another clue: On the page for Trump's Doral golf resort, near Miami, users posted photos from inside the club. One of them appears to show Schanz's painting, hanging on a wall at the resort. The date on the photo was February 2016.

David Fahrenthold ✓
@Fahrenthold

Shout-out to the anonymous law prof. who pointed this out to me when I -- clueless -- called abt something else. You know who you are!

David Fahrenthold @Fahrenthold
NY AG says @realdonaldtrump's Fdn in violation of law, orders it to stop raising $ or be deemed "continuing fraud." wpo.st/qsD22

RETWEETS   LIKES
767   1,965

1:00 PM - 3 Oct 2016

↩ 56   ⟲ 767   ♥ 2K

Trump Foundation ordered to stop fundraising by N.Y. attorney general's office

By David A. Fahrenthold
Oct. 3, 2016

THE NEW YORK ATTORNEY GENERAL DISCLOSED MONDAY that it ordered Donald Trump's personal charity to cease fundraising immediately after determining that the foundation was violating state law by soliciting donations without proper authorization.

The message was conveyed in a "notice of violation" sent Friday to the Donald J. Trump Foundation, of which Trump is president.

The night before, The Washington Post reported that Trump's foundation — which has subsisted entirely on other people's donations since 2008 — had failed to register with the state as a charity soliciting money.

Because of that, Trump's foundation had avoided rigorous annual audits that New York state requires of

Donald Trump's foundation, because it didn't have the proper fundraising authorization, avoided annual audits that New York state requires of charities that seek the public's money. (Molly Riley/AFP/Getty Images)

charities that seek the public's money. Those audits would have asked, among other things, if the foundation's money had been used to benefit Trump or one of his businesses.

"The Trump Foundation must immediately cease soliciting contributions or engaging in any other fundraising activities in New York," wrote James G. Sheehan, the head of the charities bureau in the office of Attorney General Eric Schneiderman (D).

In addition, Sheehan wrote, the Trump Foundation was ordered to supply the state with all the legal paperwork necessary to register as a charity that solicits money within 15 days.

Trump's foundation must also look back and determine whether it violated state law in prior years by soliciting money without authorization, Sheehan wrote. If so, it must provide the financial audit reports it should have provided for those years. Those reports, Sheehan said, are also due within 15 days.

If Trump's foundation does not comply, Sheehan wrote, it will be considered "a continuing fraud upon the people of New York."

Trump campaign spokeswoman Hope Hicks responded in a written statement: "While we remain very concerned about the political motives behind AG Schneiderman's investigation, the Trump Foundation nevertheless intends to cooperate fully with the investigation. Because this is an ongoing legal matter, the Trump Foundation will not comment further at this time."

Schneiderman has endorsed Democrat Hillary Clinton, Trump's rival in the presidential race.

Last month, his office launched a broader probe of the Trump Foundation after stories in The Post identified cases in which Trump appeared to have used the charity's money to buy portraits of himself and to settle lawsuits involving his for-profit businesses. In addition, Trump's foundation gave a $25,000 gift to a campaign committee supporting Florida Attorney General Pam Bondi (R). Nonprofits such as the Trump Foundation are prohibited from giving political gifts.

Legal experts said the move to suspend the Trump Foundation's ability to raise money is a common reaction in cases in which a charity has solicited funds without authorization.

"You have to register with the attorney general if you're going to raise money from the public. And they're not doing it. So this would happen to anybody," said Daniel

Kurtz, a lawyer in private practice who previously oversaw the New York attorney general's charities bureau.

"I think this is probably pretty close to a form letter," Kurtz said of the notice sent to Trump's foundation.

Trump started his foundation in 1987 to give away the proceeds from his book "The Art of the Deal." It has no paid employees and a board of five: Trump, three of his children and a longtime Trump Organization employee. They all work a half-hour per week, according to the foundation's most recent Internal Revenue Service filing.

For years, Trump himself was the Trump Foundation's only source of money: Between 1987 and 2006, he donated $5.4 million.

But by the end of 2006, Trump had given away almost all the money he had put in — leaving just $4,238 in the foundation's coffers. His giving abruptly shrank and then dried up: Trump gave $35,000 in 2007, $30,000 in 2008 and then no donations at all after that, tax records show.

Instead, Trump's name-branded charity has been sustained entirely by other people's money. Some of those donors have not said whether Trump himself solicited their gifts.

Vince and Linda McMahon, the pro-wrestling executives, have given a total of $5 million and have declined to comment. NBCUniversal, which televised Trump's reality show, "The Apprentice," has declined to explain the reason behind its $500,000 gift in 2012.

But in other cases, there is evidence that Trump was involved in asking for the money or directing it to the foundation.

There was a $100,000 gift from Norwegian Cruise

Lines in 2005, after Trump's wife, Melania, served as "god-mother" to a new ship. A spokeswoman for the cruise line said the Trumps helped arrange a donation to the Trump Foundation as part of that deal.

In 2011, Donald Trump appeared on a televised "roast" on Comedy Central and directed that his $400,000 appearance fee be sent to the Trump Foundation.

Trump's foundation has also received about $1.9 million from a New York businessman named Richard Ebers, who sells high-end tickets and once-in-a-lifetime experiences to wealthy clients. Two people familiar with that arrangement said Ebers owed Trump for goods and services he had purchased — and was instructed to pay Trump's foundation instead.

The Trump Foundation made its most wide-ranging request for donations earlier this year. After a fundraiser that Trump held for veterans in Iowa, the foundation set up a public website, www.donaldtrumpforvets.com. It took donations via credit card, and Trump said they would be passed on to veterans' groups.

Under New York law, the foundation was supposed to obtain a special registration before it solicited gifts from the public. The law's definition of "solicit" was quite broad: "to directly or indirectly make a request for a contribution, whether express or implied, through any medium."

The state requires any charity that solicits $25,000 or more per year in New York to register under a provision called "7A," for its article heading.

The most significant consequence, for a charity of the Trump Foundation's size, would have been a requirement that it submit to annual audits by outside accountants. Trump's charity never did.

Trump's campaign has not said anything about why. Earlier this fall, Trump implied that he had trusted lawyers to run the foundation properly.

"Well, I hope so," he said, when asked whether the foundation had followed the law. "I mean, my lawyers do it."

But the Trump Foundation has reported spending very little on legal fees — at least, before this year. Between 1990 and 2014, the most recent year for which tax records are available, the foundation spent a total of $211 on lawyers.

Sean Sullivan in Pueblo, Colo., contributed to this report.

David Fahrenthold ✓
@Fahrenthold

stand by for some news about
@realDonaldTrump....

RETWEETS	LIKES
200	1,323

3:02 PM - 7 Oct 2016

↩ 116   ⇄ 200   ♥ 1.3K

Trump recorded having extremely lewd conversation about women in 2005

By David A. Fahrenthold
Oct. 7, 2016

DONALD TRUMP BRAGGED IN VULGAR TERMS ABOUT KISS-ing, groping and trying to have sex with women during a 2005 conversation caught on a hot microphone, saying that "when you're a star, they let you do it," according to a video obtained by The Washington Post.

The video captures Trump talking with Billy Bush, then of "Access Hollywood," on a bus with the show's name written across the side. They were arriving on the set of "Days of Our Lives" to tape a segment about Trump's cameo on the soap opera.

Late Friday night, following sharp criticism by Republican leaders, Trump issued a short video statement saying, "I said it, I was wrong, and I apologize." But he also called the revelation "a distraction from the issues we are facing today." He said that his "foolish" words are much different than the words and actions of Bill Clinton, whom he accused of abusing women, and Hillary Clinton, whom he accused of having "bullied, attacked, shamed and intimidated his victims."

"I've never said I'm a perfect person, nor pretended to be someone that I'm not. I've said and done things I regret, and the words released today on this more than a decade-old video are one of them. Anyone who knows me knows these words don't reflect who I am," Trump said.

In an apparent response to Republican critics asking him to drop out of the race, he said: "We will discuss this more in the coming days. See you at the debate on Sunday."

The tape includes audio of Bush and Trump talking inside the bus, as well as audio and video once they emerge from it to begin shooting the segment.

In that audio, Trump discusses a failed attempt to seduce a woman, whose full name is not given in the video.

"I moved on her, and I failed. I'll admit it," Trump is heard saying. It was unclear when the events he was describing took place. The tape was recorded several months after he married his third wife, Melania.

"Whoa," another voice said.

"I did try and f--- her. She was married," Trump says.

Trump continues: "And I moved on her very heavily. In fact, I took her out furniture shopping. She wanted to get some furniture. I said, 'I'll show you where they have some nice furniture.'"

"I moved on her like a bitch, but I couldn't get there. And she was married," Trump says. "Then all of a sudden

I see her, she's now got the big phony tits and everything. She's totally changed her look."

At that point in the audio, Trump and Bush appear to notice Arianne Zucker, the actress who is waiting to escort them into the soap-opera set.

"Your girl's hot as s---, in the purple," says Bush, who's now a co-host of NBC's "Today" show.

"Whoa!" Trump says. "Whoa!"

"I've got to use some Tic Tacs, just in case I start kissing her," Trump says. "You know I'm automatically attracted to beautiful — I just start kissing them. It's like a magnet. Just kiss. I don't even wait."

"And when you're a star, they let you do it," Trump says. "You can do anything."

"Whatever you want," says another voice, apparently Bush's.

"Grab them by the p---y," Trump says. "You can do anything."

A spokeswoman for NBC Universal, which produces and distributes "Access Hollywood," declined to comment.

"This was locker-room banter, a private conversation that took place many years ago. Bill Clinton has said far worse to me on the golf course — not even close," Trump said in a statement. "I apologize if anyone was offended."

Billy Bush, in a statement released by NBC Universal, said: "Obviously I'm embarrassed and ashamed. It's no excuse, but this happened eleven years ago — I was younger, less mature, and acted foolishly in playing along. I'm very sorry."

After the video appeared online Friday afternoon, Democratic nominee Hillary Clinton wrote on Twitter:

"This is horrific. We cannot allow this man to become president." Her running mate, Sen. Tim Kaine (Va.), told reporters, "It makes me sick to my stomach," while campaigning in Las Vegas.

Planned Parenthood Action Fund, which has endorsed Clinton, issued a statement from Executive Vice President Dawn Laguens saying: "What Trump described in these tapes amounts to sexual assault."

Trump was also criticized by members of his own party. House Speaker Paul D. Ryan, who said he is "sickened" by Trump's comments, said the Republican presidential candidate will no longer appear with him at a campaign event in Wisconsin on Saturday.

"Women are to be championed and revered, not objectified. I hope Mr. Trump treats this situation with the seriousness it deserves and works to demonstrate to the country that he has greater respect for women than this clip suggests," Ryan said in a statement.

In a short statement issued moments after Ryan's, Trump said his running mate, Indiana Gov. Mike Pence, "will be representing me" at the Wisconsin event.

Sen. Kelly Ayotte (N.H.), who is running for reelection and has said she will vote for Trump, called his comments "totally inappropriate and offensive."

Republican National Committee Chairman Reince Priebus, who has stood by Trump uncritically through numerous controversies, said in a statement: "No woman should ever be described in these terms or talked about in this manner. Ever."

Former presidential candidate Mitt Romney, a Trump critic, said in a statement: "Hitting on married women?

Condoning assault? Such vile degradations demean our wives and daughters and corrupt America's face to the world."

Senate Majority Leader Mitch McConnell (R-Ky.) said the comments are "repugnant, and unacceptable in any circumstance" and made clear Trump's brief statement would not suffice.

"As the father of three daughters, I strongly believe that Trump needs to apologize directly to women and girls everywhere, and take full responsibility for the utter lack of respect for women shown in his comments on that tape," he said late Friday.

One of Trump's most prominent social-conservative supporters, Tony Perkins of the Family Research Council, told BuzzFeed's Rosie Gray: "My personal support for Donald Trump has never been based upon shared values."

Trump's running mate, Pence, was at a diner in Toledo when the news broke — about to view the diner's collection of signed cardboard hot-dog buns, which includes one signed by Trump. But the reporters traveling with Pence were quickly ushered out of the diner by campaign staff, before they could ask Trump's running mate about it, according to Politico. Politico reported that the journalists, traveling in Pence's "protective pool," were not permitted to film Pence as he left the diner.

The tape appears at a time when Trump, the Republican presidential nominee, has sought to make a campaign issue out of his opponent's marriage. Trump has criticized former president Bill Clinton for his past infidelity and criticized opponent Hillary Clinton as her husband's "enabler."

"Hillary Clinton was married to the single greatest

abuser of women in the history of politics," Trump told the New York Times in a recent interview. "Hillary was an enabler, and she attacked the women who Bill Clinton mistreated afterward. I think it's a serious problem for them, and it's something that I'm considering talking about more in the near future."

Trump carried on a very public affair with Marla Maples — his eventual second wife — while still married to first wife Ivana Trump.

Trump has been criticized in this campaign for derogatory and lewd comments about women, including some made on TV and live radio. In an interview Wednesday with KSNV, a Las Vegas television station, Trump said that those comments were made for entertainment.

"A lot of that was done for the purpose of entertainment. There's nobody that has more respect for women than I do," he told the station.

"Are you trying to tone it down now?" asked the interviewer, Jim Snyder.

"It's not a question of trying, it's very easy," Trump said.

The tape obtained by The Post seems to have captured Trump in a private moment, with no audience beyond Bush and a few others on the bus. It appears to have been shot around Sept. 16, 2005, which was the day media reports said Trump would tape his soap-opera cameo.

The video shows the bus carrying Trump and Bush turning down a street on the studio back lot. The two men cannot be seen.

"Oh, nice legs, huh?" Trump says.

"Oof, get out of the way, honey," Bush says, apparently referencing somebody else blocking the view of Zucker.

The two men then exit the bus and greet Zucker.

"We're ready, let's go," Trump says, after the initial greetings. "Make me a soap star."

"How about a little hug for the Donald?" Bush says. "He just got off the bus."

"Would you like a little hug, darling?" Zucker says.

"Absolutely," Trump says. As they embrace, and air-kiss, Trump says, "Melania said this was okay."

The video then follows Trump, Bush and Zucker into the studio. Trump did appear on "Days of Our Lives" in late October. In a tape of that cameo posted online, Zucker's character asks Trump — playing himself — for a job at his business, and tells him suggestively, "I think you'll find I'm a very willing employee. Working under you, I think, could be mutually beneficial."

Trump's character gives her the brushoff.

"That's an interesting proposition," Trump says on-screen. "I'll get back to you."

A publicist for Zucker did not immediately respond to questions on Friday afternoon.

Rosalind S. Helderman, Mike DeBonis, Jenna Johnson and Sarah Parnass contributed to this report.

First, though, take a look at this picture of @realdonaldtrump and Giuliani doing the Macarena. It will be important later.

Trump boasts about his philanthropy. But his giving falls short of his words.

By David A. Fahrenthold
Oct. 29, 2016

IN THE FALL OF 1996, A CHARITY CALLED THE ASSOCIATION to Benefit Children held a ribbon-cutting in Manhattan for a new nursery school serving children with AIDS. The bold-faced names took seats up front.

There was then-Mayor Rudolph W. Giuliani (R) and former mayor David Dinkins (D). TV stars Frank and Kathie Lee Gifford, who were major donors. And there was a seat saved for Steven Fisher, a developer who had given generously to build the nursery.

Then, all of a sudden, there was Donald Trump.

"Nobody knew he was coming," said Abigail Disney, another donor sitting on the dais. "There's this kind of ruckus at the door, and I don't know what was going on, and in comes Donald Trump. [He] just gets up on the podium and sits down."

Trump was not a major donor. He was not a donor, period. He'd never given a dollar to the nursery or the Association to Benefit Children, according to Gretchen Buchenholz, the charity's executive director then and now.

But now he was sitting in Fisher's seat, next to Giuliani.

"Frank Gifford turned to me and said, 'Why is he here?'" Buchenholz recalled recently. By then, the ceremony had begun. There was nothing to do.

"Just sing past it," she recalled Gifford telling her.

So they warbled into the first song on the program, "This Little Light of Mine," alongside Trump and a chorus of children — with a photographer snapping photos, and Trump looking for all the world like an honored donor to the cause.

Afterward, Disney and Buchenholz recalled, Trump left without offering an explanation. Or a donation. Fisher was stuck in the audience. The charity spent months trying to repair its relationship with him.

"I mean, what's wrong with you, man?" Disney recalled thinking of Trump, when it was over.

For as long as he has been rich and famous, Donald Trump has also wanted people to believe he is generous. He spent years constructing an image as a philanthropist by appearing at charity events and by making very public — even nationally televised — promises to give his own money away.

It was, in large part, a facade. A months-long investigation by The Washington Post has not been able to verify many of Trump's boasts about his philanthropy.

Instead, throughout his life in the spotlight, whether as a businessman, television star or presidential candidate, The Post found that Trump had sought credit for charity he had not given — or had claimed other people's giving as his own.

It is impossible to know for certain what Trump has given to charity, because he has declined to release his tax returns. In all, The Post was able to identify $7.8 million in charitable giving from Trump's own pocket since the early 1980s.

In public appearances, Trump often made it appear that he gave far more.

Trump promised to give away the proceeds of Trump University. He promised to donate the salary he earned from "The Apprentice." He promised to give personal donations to the charities chosen by contestants on "Celebrity Apprentice." He promised to donate $250,000 to a charity helping Israeli soldiers and veterans.

Together, those pledges would have increased Trump's lifetime giving by millions of dollars. But The Post has been unable to verify that he followed through on any of them.

Instead, The Post found that his personal giving has almost disappeared entirely in recent years. After calling 420-plus charities with some connection to Trump, The Post found only one personal gift from Trump between 2008 and the spring of this year. That was a gift to the Police Athletic League of New York City, in 2009. It was worth less than $10,000.

The charity that Trump has given the most money to over his lifetime appears to be his own: the Donald J. Trump Foundation.

But that charity, too, was not what it seemed.

The Trump Foundation appeared outwardly to be a typical, if small, philanthropic foundation — set up by a rich man to give his riches away.

In reality, it has been funded largely by other people. Tax records show the Trump Foundation has received $5.5 million from Trump over its life, and nothing since 2008. It received $9.3 million from other people.

Another unusual feature: One of the foundation's most consistent causes was Trump himself.

New findings, for instance, show that the Trump Foundation's largest-ever gift — $264,631 — was used to renovate a fountain outside the windows of Trump's Plaza Hotel.

Its smallest-ever gift, for $7, was paid to the Boy Scouts in 1989, at a time when it cost $7 to register a new Scout. Trump's oldest son was 11 at the time. Trump did not respond to a question about whether the money was paid to register him.

At other times, Trump used his foundation's funds to settle legal disputes involving Trump's for-profit companies and to buy two large portraits of himself, including one that wound up hanging on the wall of the sports bar at a Trump-owned golf resort. Those purchases raised questions about whether Trump had violated laws against "self-dealing" by charity leaders.

In advance of this article, The Post sent more than 70 questions to the Trump campaign.

Those questions covered the individual anecdotes and statistics contained in this article, including the tale about

Trump crashing the ribbon-cutting in 1996, as well as broader questions about Trump's life as a philanthropist.

Exactly when, before this spring, did Trump last give his own money to charity?

What did Trump consider his greatest act of charity in recent years?

Trump's campaign did not respond until Saturday afternoon, after this article was published online; it sent a written statement saying that Trump "has personally donated tens of millions of dollars ... to charitable causes."

Trump officials did not respond when asked to provide evidence of the tens of millions of dollars in gifts.

The result of The Post's examination of Trump's charity is a portrait of the GOP nominee, revealed in the negative space between what he was willing to promise — and what he was willing to give.

"All of this is completely consistent with who Trump is. He's a man who operates inside a tiny bubble that never extends beyond what he believes is his self-interest," said Tony Schwartz, Trump's co-author on his 1987 book "The Art of the Deal." Schwartz has become a fierce critic of Trump in this election.

"If your worldview is only you — if all you're seeing is a mirror — then there's nobody to give money to," Schwartz said. "Except yourself."

'AN ARDENT PHILANTHROPIST'

In several interviews with The Post this year, Trump has declined to supply details about his giving, saying that if

Donald Trump presents a check to members of Support Siouxland Soldiers in late January at the Orpheum Theatre in Sioux City, Iowa. At right is Jerry Falwell Jr., president of Liberty University. (Patrick Semansky/AP)

charities knew what Trump had donated they would badger him to give more.

"I give mostly to a lot of different groups," Trump said in one interview.

"Can you give us any names?" asked The Post's Drew Harwell in May.

"No, I don't want to. No, I don't want to," Trump responded. "I'd like to keep it private."

Of the $7.8 million in personal giving that The Post identified, about 70 percent — $5.5 million — went to the Trump Foundation, which was founded in 1987. All of that giving came before 2009; since then, the foundation's tax records show no donations at all from Trump to his foundation. Its coffers have been filled by others, including $5 million from pro-wrestling executives Vince and Linda McMahon.

At least $1.1 million of Trump's giving has come in the last six months.

That includes a gift that first brought Trump's charity — and the gap between the promises and the substance of his giving — to the center of his presidential campaign.

In January, Trump skipped a GOP primary debate in a feud with Fox News and held a televised fundraiser for veterans. In that broadcast, Trump said he'd personally donated to the cause: "Donald Trump gave $1 million," he said.

Months later, The Post could find no evidence Trump had done so. Then, Corey Lewandowski — Trump's campaign manager at the time — called to say the money had been given out. In private. No details. "He's not going to share that information," Lewandowski said.

In reality, at that point, Trump had given nothing.

Trump didn't give away the $1 million until a few days later, as the news media sought to check Lewandowski's false claim. Trump gave it all to the Marine Corps-Law Enforcement Foundation, which helps families of fallen Marines. Trump bristled at this reporter's suggestion that he had given the money away only because the media were asking about it.

"You know, you're a nasty guy. You're really a nasty guy," Trump said. "I gave out millions of dollars that I had no obligation to do."

Later, in August, Trump also gave $100,000 to a church near Baton Rouge. He sent the check after visiting the church during a tour of flood-ravaged areas.

For years, Trump built a reputation as somebody whose charity was as big as his success.

That identity was expressed, for a time, in Trump's biography on his corporate website. His image had two seemingly equal parts.

"He is the archetypal businessman," the biography said, "a deal maker without peer and an ardent philanthropist."

In the books he wrote or co-wrote about himself, Trump frequently praised charitable giving in the abstract — casting it as a moral response to his vast wealth.

"We've benefited from the American Dream and we feel the duty to give back to the community," he wrote of his family in "The America We Deserve" in 2000. "Those who don't are nothing more than parasites."

In the same books, Trump seemed to regard charity differently when he encountered it in his day-to-day life.

In those cases, it sounds like a hassle.

A game he can't win, and hates playing.

"The people who run charities know that I've got wealthy friends and can get them to buy tables," Trump said in "The Art of the Deal," explaining why he'd turned down a charity request from New York Yankee Dave Winfield. "I understand the game, and while I don't like to play it, there is no graceful way out."

One rare time when Trump describes finding joy in the act of charity comes in 2008's "Trump: Never Give Up."

"I can remember a friend who asked me why I had so many charity events at my properties," Trump wrote. "I said to him, 'Because I can!'... It's a great feeling, and it makes all the work that goes into acquiring all those beautiful properties and buildings worth it."

But that's not entirely a story about how Trump gives money away.

It's also a story about how Trump makes money.

Charities pay him to rent out his clubs and banquet rooms for fundraiser galas. At the Mar-a-Lago Club in Palm Beach, they can pay $275,000 or more for a single night. Sometimes, Trump has given donations from the Trump Foundation to the charities that are his customers.

But in some of those cases, he still comes out ahead.

"It cost, I think, 20-some thousand," said William Hertzler, of the German-American Hall of Fame, who rented space at Trump Tower when the hall inducted Trump in 2012. Trump was the 15th person inducted, the year after magicians Siegfried and Roy. Trump gave a $1,000 donation from the Trump Foundation.

Hertzler said the hall of fame was okay with that. "He came down" to attend the gala, held in the same tower where Trump lives, Hertzler said. "His time is very valuable."

'ADVANCING TRUMP'S INTERESTS'

In his early days as a developer — when he was a New York celebrity but not yet a national one — Trump made some high-profile personal gifts to charity. He gave $1 million to a Manhattan Vietnam Veterans' memorial in 1983. Then, after taking over the renovation of the city-owned Wollman Rink in Central Park, Trump said he donated some of its proceeds to charities.

But, even then, Trump was looking for ways to have other people support his charitable causes.

Donald Trump with New York City's Park Commissioner Henry Stern, left, holding ice skates that were intended for use at the Wollman Skating Rink Central Park in New York on Aug. 7, 1986. (G. Paul Burnett/Associated Press)

"He wanted me to get as much money as I could from the contractors. And I was a good soldier, and so I went out and put the arm round them [saying], 'I need you to buy a table at the United Cerebral Palsy gala,'" said Barbara Res, a longtime Trump employee who recalled being sent out on job sites in advance of charity galas hosted by Trump's then-wife Ivana.

Usually, Res said, the contractors paid. "They whined. And I pushed."

Then, in 1987 Trump published "The Art of the Deal."

He became a national celebrity — and made his charity a key part of his brand.

"I don't do it for the money. I've got enough, more than I'll ever need," Trump wrote on the book's first page.

So, Trump said in interviews, if he made money off the

book in which he wrote he didn't need money, he would give it to charity.

"To the homeless, to Vietnam veterans, for AIDS, multiple sclerosis," Trump told the New York Times two years later. "Originally, I figured they'd get a couple of hundred thousand, but because of the success of 'The Art of the Deal,' they'll get four or five million."

So in 1987, Trump signed the forms to incorporate the Donald J. Trump Foundation. The paperwork warned that he could not use the charity's money to help political candidates. Nor could he use it for the benefit of "any member, trustee, director or officer" of the charity.

That first year, Trump made himself president.

He put in $144,050.

Then he used $100 of the foundation's money to buy a two-person membership to the Metropolitan Museum of Art.

Trump did not respond to a question about whether the membership was for his own use. If it was, it may have been a violation of the laws against "self-dealing."

"You've got to pay for it yourself; you can't have your foundation pay for it," said Lloyd Mayer, a professor teaching tax law at Notre Dame Law School. He said this payment, small as it was, appeared to provide a benefit directly to Trump. In which case Trump — not the charity — should have paid.

In the foundation's first four years, Trump put in a total of $1.9 million, proceeds from the best-selling book and from the poor-selling "Trump, The Game."

He was the Trump Foundation's only donor.

Though that was not for lack of trying.

"If you could ask your accountants to write a check to the 'Donald J. Trump Foundation,' I will distribute the money in my name and yours and will let you have a list of the charities which benefitted," Trump wrote in a letter to boxer Mike Tyson in 1988, according to news reports from the time.

Trump had helped Tyson with business dealings and believed Tyson owed him $2 million. He wanted it to go to the Trump Foundation instead. That doesn't seem to have happened — tax records show no donations from Tyson.

The largest donation in the history of the Trump Foundation was made in 1989. The Central Park Conservancy wanted to restore the Pulitzer Fountain, a turned-off, crumbling feature next to the famous park. The city wouldn't pay for it, saying the money was needed elsewhere.

So owners of the 15 buildings around the fountain — who would benefit directly from its restoration — were asked to pay a voluntary "tax." The tax was $0.50 per square foot.

At the time, Trump owned one of those 15 buildings: the Plaza Hotel. Its front door faced the fountain.

Today, the Plaza is about 1 million square feet.

If it was the same in the 1980s — hotel officials weren't sure — that would have led to a tax of $500,000 or so.

The conservancy's records show that Trump's hotel paid some of the "tax" — between $100,000 and $250,000 — in 1988.

In 1989, the Trump Foundation also paid $264,631 to the Central Park Conservancy. It appeared that Trump's charity had contributed to an effort that enhanced the view outside Trump's business.

"It shows you what this [foundation] is all about. Which is basically just about advancing Trump's interests," said Brian Galle, a professor of tax law at Georgetown University. The Central Park Conservancy declined to comment.

In 1990, Trump's businesses started to go south, plunging him into a period of heavy debt. In 1991, his creditors limited his living expenses to $375,000 a month.

At that time, Trump's giving to charity collapsed. He gave $0 to the Trump Foundation in 1991. Around the same year, Trump tried again to get somebody else to pay his charitable donations for him.

In late 1990, the all-female band Precious Metal was going to shoot a video for their remake of "Mr. Big Stuff." Trump made headlines by agreeing to star as the title character, in return for a charitable donation.

"I want to give it to my favorite charity, and it's just 10 grand," Leslie Knauer, the lead singer for the band, recalled Trump saying.

They shot the video, Knauer said.

Then, a few days later, the band got a call.

"You know, $10,000 really isn't a Trump kind of donation," Trump said, according to interviews Knauer gave at the time. He wanted $250,000.

The move backfired. The band re-shot the video with a look-alike. Knauer said they gave Trump nothing.

"Then he said [publicly] he hated the song," Knauer recalled. "It was horrible."

In that low period of Trump's finances, his generosity dried up even to those close to him.

For instance, Res — the executive who had spent years leaning on Trump's contractors to buy tables at his wife's fundraisers — came to Trump to ask for a favor of her own.

"I got an award from a group called the Professional Women in Construction," she recalled. There was a gala. There were tables. She'd sold a number to subcontractors she knew.

But, usually, the winning woman's employer was the big spender, buying multiple tables or paying for high-level sponsorships. That was Trump.

He didn't.

"He showed up at the door and bought one ticket," said Lenore Janis, the leader of the Professional Women in Construction at the time. The ticket cost $100.

"And then he said to me, the president of the organization, 'I have a few things that I want to say. I will need the microphone,'" Janis said.

She said no. But Trump found somebody who said yes. "He got up there and for 15 minutes he blew his own horn," Janis said, so that anybody watching would think he'd written a big check.

Afterward, Janis said her son photocopied the check and hung it on his wall.

"Oh, my God, a check signed by Mr. Trump!" Janis recalled him saying. "And I said, 'It should have been, like, $20,000. ... Grow up.'"

Donald Trump, alongside New Jersey Gov. Chris Christie, left, speaks at a campaign event at the Mar-A-Lago Club in Palm Beach, Fla., on March 1, 2016. (Jabin Botsford/The Washington Post)

'THE MOST CLUELESS PERSON'

As the 1990s went on, Trump's finances slowly climbed out of the red.

And in 1995, he made one of the most famous charitable gestures of his life.

That year Trump gave a donation to help finance a Manhattan parade honoring veterans on the 50th anniversary of the end of World War II.

At the time, press reports pegged his gift at $200,000. In recent interviews, one of the organizers said he thought it was higher, closer to $500,000.

"He certainly put his money where his mouth was, and he certainly helped us when we were in pretty bad shape," said Vince McGowan, who helped organize the event.

Trump, who had obtained five deferments to avoid

the Vietnam-era draft, was named a grand marshal, and he marched near the front of the huge column of veterans. He was later honored with an invitation to visit the Pentagon and meet the Joint Chiefs of Staff.

Trump describes this gift in his most recent book, called "Great Again: How to Fix Our Crippled America."

"I donated a one-million-dollar matching grant," he wrote.

As the 1990s went on, Trump also increased his giving to the Trump Foundation: $6,500 in 1992, $8,500 in 1993, then $74,432 in 1994, after Trump said he'd sold photos of his wedding to Marla Maples and given the proceeds to his charity.

As it rose again, the Trump Foundation continued to be used to benefit its namesake.

The best illustration of that was the charity to which the foundation gave its two largest gifts of the 1990s. The Trump Foundation gave $50,000 in 1995, and another $50,000 in 1999, to a nonprofit called the National Museum of Catholic Art and History.

Those gifts, not previously reported, seemed like an odd choice for big charitable dollars.

The museum was housed for much of the 1990s in a former headquarters for "Fat Tony" Salerno of the Genovese crime family in East Harlem. It had few visitors and little art. A Village Voice reporter, visiting in 2001, said the collection included a photo of the pope, some nun dolls bought from the Home Shopping Network, and — just off the dining room — "a black Jacuzzi decorated with simmering candles, gold-plated soap dishes, and kitsch angel figurines."

Trump is not Catholic.

But he and the museum had a mutual friend.

Ed Malloy, who was then the chairman of the museum's board, was the head of the powerful labor group, the Building and Construction Trades Council.News reports from the time indicate that he was a business ally of Trump's: Union members worked on Trump buildings, and Malloy helped Trump line up vital financing from a union pension fund.

"Contributing to this museum — you know, it only made sense in the context of relationships," said Wayne Barrett, the Village Voice reporter, in a recent interview.

The Trump campaign did not respond to requests for comment about these donations.

Malloy died in 2012.

The Catholic museum shut down in 2010.

"I cannot give you a comment. I don't want to be quoted on anything," said Christina Cox, the museum's former director, when The Post reached her by phone.

At times, Trump seemed to make light of others' expectations about his generosity.

In 1997, for instance, he was "principal for a day" at a public school in an impoverished area of the Bronx. The chess team was holding a bake sale, Hot & Crusty danishes and croissants. They were $5,000 short of what they needed to travel to a tournament.

Trump had brought something to wow them.

"He handed them a fake million-dollar bill," said David MacEnulty, a teacher and the chess team's coach.

The team's parent volunteers were thrilled.

Then disappointment.

Trump then gave them $200 in real money and drove away in a limousine.

Why just $200?

"I have no idea," MacEnulty said. "He was about the most clueless person I've ever seen in that regard."

The happy ending, he said, was that a woman read about Trump's gift in the New York Times, called the school and donated the $5,000. "I am ashamed to be the same species as this man," MacEnulty recalled her saying.

At a nursery school a year earlier, Trump had crashed the ribbon-cutting for the event aimed at helping children with AIDS.

Once he was onstage, Trump played the part of a big donor convincingly. Photos from the event show Trump smiling, right behind Giuliani, as the mayor cut the ribbon. During the "celebratory dance" segment of the program, Trump mugged and did the macarena with Giuliani, Kathie Lee Gifford and a group of children.

"I am just heartsick," Buchenholz, the executive director, wrote the next day to the donor whose seat Trump had taken. Buchenholz provided a copy of the email.

"I immediately said 'no,' but Rudy Giuliani said 'yes' and I felt I had to accede to him," Buchenholz wrote. "I hope you can forgive me." Buchenholz said that Fisher did remain a donor, despite the snub.

Trump and Giuliani did not respond to questions about the event.

A spokeswoman for Fisher said he did not recall it.

Buchenholz said her group did not receive any donations from Trump until three years later. The charity was holding a gala on a cruise ship. Trump bought tickets and paid with $2,000 from the Trump Foundation.

'UNUSUAL AND ALARMING'

If Trump had never run for president, the cost of his charitable shortfalls would only have fallen on his conscience.

He had not, apparently, faced any kind of scrutiny for the way he ran the Trump Foundation. Former IRS officials say that's not surprising. They said the IRS largely relies on the honor system: It asks charities to flag their own bad behavior, reporting if they made a prohibited political gift or committed an act of self-dealing.

The Trump Foundation never did.

"So it was invisible," said Marc S. Owens, the former longtime head of the IRS office dealing with nonprofits.

During his run for president, Trump has faced new consequences.

Trump paid a $2,500 penalty tax, after The Post reported that his foundation had made a political gift in 2013 to a committee aiding Florida Attorney General Pamela Bondi (R).

Also, earlier this month, New York Attorney General Eric Schneiderman (D) ordered the Trump Foundation to cease its fundraising — after The Post revealed that it had been soliciting funds from the public without obtaining a special registration required by state law.

Schneiderman's office is also investigating the Trump Foundation, examining its acts of possible self-dealing. In a written statement, Schneiderman called reports about the foundation "unusual and alarming."

Tax-law experts said it's possible that the Trump Foundation will be — or perhaps already is — under investigation by the IRS. The IRS has declined to comment.

Trump also has faced political attacks from Clinton and other Democrats, who have mocked his foundation as evidence of his character.

"The Trump Foundation ... took money from other people and bought a six-foot portrait of Donald," Clinton said during the third presidential debate. "I mean, who does that?" she said.

Trump's response was that, in effect, it could have been worse.

At least he didn't buy something more expensive than a painting.

"Trump Foundation, small foundation. People contribute, I contribute. The money goes 100 percent — 100 percent goes to different charities, including a lot of military," Trump said. "I don't get anything. I don't buy boats. I don't buy planes."

The next night, Trump and Clinton were together again, this time in Manhattan at the Alfred E. Smith dinner, which benefits Catholic charities.

In the program for that event, Trump's official biography echoed the language he had used about himself for years.

Despite all that had been revealed about his charitable giving during the course of his campaign, Trump stuck with the old self-image. He was a man whose identity had two equally important sides.

"Mr. Trump is the archetypal businessman," the bio said, "a deal maker without peer and an ardent philanthropist."

Alice Crites contributed to this report.

David Fahrenthold ✔
@Fahrenthold

.@AGSchneiderman Will your investigation of Trump Fdn continue, now that @realDonaldTrump aides have said he plans to shut it down?

RETWEETS LIKES
281   670

1:44 PM - 24 Dec 2016

↩ 41   ⟲ 281   ♥ 670

Donald Trump plans to shut down his charitable foundation, which has been under scrutiny for months

By Mark Berman and David A. Fahrenthold

Dec. 24, 2016

PRESIDENT-ELECT DONALD TRUMP SAID HE PLANS TO SHUT down his charitable foundation, a decision that comes after repeated controversies over how it collected and disbursed funds.

In a statement Saturday, Trump offered no timeline for when his foundation would close down but said he had directed his attorney to take the steps needed to close it. It was not immediately clear when the foundation would be able to dissolve, given an ongoing investigation in New York.

"The Foundation has done enormous good works over the years in contributing millions of dollars to countless worthy groups, including supporting veterans, law enforcement officers and children," Trump said in the statement. "However, to avoid even the appearance of any conflict with my role as President I have decided to continue to pursue my strong interest in philanthropy in other ways."

The Donald J. Trump Foundation has come under intense scrutiny this year after a series of reports in The Washington Post detailing its practices, including cases in which Trump apparently used the charity's money to settle lawsuits involving his for-profit businesses.

New York's attorney general has been investigating the charity after some of these reports, and a spokeswoman for that office said the foundation could not officially shut down until that probe is over.

"The Trump Foundation is still under investigation by this office and cannot legally dissolve until that investigation is complete," Amy Spitalnick, the spokeswoman, said in an email Saturday.

The foundation is unusual in that it largely collects and donates money from other people. In fact, from 2009 to 2014, Trump told the Internal Revenue Service that he had given his namesake foundation no money at all. The biggest donors in recent years were Vince and Linda McMahon, the pro-wrestling moguls, who gave the Trump Foundation $5 million between 2007 and 2009. Trump recently nominated Linda McMahon to head the Small Business Administration.

Trump said Saturday that he was "very proud of the fact that the Foundation has operated at essentially no cost for decades, with 100% of the money going to charity." The Trump Foundation has no paid employees and a board of five, consisting of Trump, three of his children and a longtime Trump Organization employee. They all work on foundation business a half-hour per week, according to an IRS filing.

The president-elect added that "because I will be devoting so much time and energy to the Presidency and solving the many problems facing our country and the world, I don't want to allow good work to be associated with a possible conflict of interest."

The foundation told the IRS it had $1.16 million in total assets by the end of 2015, the most recent tax filing available. A spokeswoman for Trump said she had no additional information Saturday regarding where any remaining money might be sent.

Trump's foundation has admitted in IRS tax filings for 2015 that it violated a prohibition against "self-dealing" that says nonprofit leaders cannot use their charity's funds to help themselves, their relatives or their businesses.

In these tax filings, the charity checked "yes" in response to a question asking whether it had transferred any income or assets to "a disqualified person" — a description that could have meant Trump, a relative or a Trump-owned business.

Trump has not said what exactly he did to violate the rule, or what he has paid the IRS in penalty taxes as a result. The IRS has not commented when asked whether it was investigating the Trump Foundation.

Trump's charity has been prohibited from fundraising by the office of New York Attorney General Eric Schneiderman (D), an action that came after The Post reported that the foundation had failed to register with the state. This meant the foundation had dodged annual audits required in the state of New York.

Schneiderman's office is also investigating the Trump Foundation after reports in The Post describing apparent cases of self-dealing that date back to 2007. The Trump Foundation spent $30,000 to buy two large portraits of Trump himself, including one that was hung up in the sports bar at a Trump-owned resort. Trump also appears to have used $258,000 of his foundation's money — legally earmarked for charitable purposes — to settle lawsuits involving two of his for-profit clubs.

In addition, the Trump foundation gave a $25,000 gift to a campaign committee backing Florida Attorney General Pam Bondi (R) even though nonprofits like the charity are not allowed to give political gifts. That gift was made as Bondi's office was considering whether to investigate fraud allegations against Trump University. A consultant who worked on Bondi's reelection effort has said that Bondi was not aware of the complaints when she solicited the donation from Trump. Ultimately, Bondi's office did not pursue those allegations.

The move to shut down Trump's foundation, first reported Saturday by the New York Times, comes as the president-elect and his family are facing intense questions regarding how they will avoid conflicts of interest while he is in the White House.

"The announcement that the Foundation will be shut down is a necessary first step for the incoming administration to avoid massive ethics problems, but it does not come close to ending the story," said Noah Bookbinder, executive director of Citizens for Responsibility and Ethics in Washington, a watchdog group aligned with allies of Hillary Clinton. The group's tips and research helped reveal some of the Trump foundation's apparent violations of the law.

In a statement, Bookbinder said that the Trump charity's "past instances of wrongdoing must be fully investigated" and called on the president-elect to "sell his businesses and take comprehensive steps to prevent conflicts of interest for him and his administration.

Trump has said his two adult sons will run his company, but he has not provided details regarding how he will extricate himself from his complex network of businesses. He postponed a news conference this month meant to address the issue and has not rescheduled it.

In another case of Trump apparently trying to wrap up lingering questions and legal issues before he takes office, he agreed to settle fraud claims against his defunct Trump University real estate seminars. A federal judge this week gave preliminary approval to a deal in which Trump would pay $25 million as part of the settlement.

Earlier this week, Trump's second-oldest son, Eric, said he was suspending his charitable foundation after facing questions about whether donors could receive special access.

The Eric Trump Foundation, founded in 2007, raises more than $1.5 million a year through a golf tournament and other events, and it passes on the bulk of its money to St. Jude Children's Research Hospital, a pediatric-cancer center in Memphis.

The president-elect was critical of the decision regarding his son's foundation, describing it as unfair in a pair of messages this week on Twitter.

"Isn't this a ridiculous shame?" the elder Trump wrote. "He loves these kids, has raised millions of dollars for them, and now must stop. Wrong answer!"

David Fahrenthold ✔
@Fahrenthold

Following ⌄

Me too!

Taylor Amey @TaylorAmey96
@Fahrenthold thank you, good sir, for such amazing reporting on your part this year. Looking forward to what comes next!

RETWEETS
53

LIKES
450

4:31 PM - 24 Dec 2016

↩ 14   ⇄ 53   ♥ 450

APPENDIX

In an effort to find proof of Trump's personal giving, The Post contacted more than 400 charities with some ties to the GOP nominee. Some got money from the Trump Foundation (■). In other cases, Trump had a personal connection (👥) to the charity or its leaders . Some were charities that DonorSearch database records (🗄) indicated he might have given to. A variety of other reasons (✳) included media mentions, gala attendance, or involvement with Trump's TV show "Celebrity Apprentice."

Charity name	Last donation
■ 9/11 Museum	Never

Trump made a $100,000 donation from his foundation to this museum just before the New York GOP primary. He has never given his own money.

■ A Better Chance	Never
👥 Abilis	No response

Trump's nephew Fred Trump III is a major fundraiser for this Connecticut charity.

Achilles International Foundation		Never
ACLU Foundation of Florida – Broward		Never

When this group honored a lawyer who is friends with Trump, he sent $325 from his foundation. Trump has never given the group his own money.

After-School Matters		No response
AHRC NYC		Never
AIDS Project Los Angeles		Never
AIDS Service Center NYC		Never
AIPAC Tomorrow Campaign		Never

Trump spoke to the influential pro-Israel lobbying group this year.

Alfred E. Smith Memorial Foundation		No comment
Algemeiner Journal		Never

This news outlet, which writes about Israel and Jewish issues around the world, gave Trump a "Liberty Award" at their annual gala. They were hopeful he would give a donation in return. He did not. Trump gave $0 from his foundation, and $0 from his own pocket.

All Faiths Restoration and Beautification Program   Records unavailable

This is the cemetery where Trump's parents, Fred and Mary, are buried.

Alliance for Lupus Research		No comment
ALS Association		No comment

In 2014, Trump made an Ice Bucket Challenge video in which two Miss Universe contestants drenched him with Trump-branded water. These videos were made as part of a fundraiser for the ALS Association. Trump's foundation gave $0 to the ALS Association that year. Did Trump give his own money? The association said it could not release that information without Trump's permission.

Alzheimer's Association		Never
Alzheimer's Community Care		Never
American Associates of Ben-Gurion University		Never
American Australian Association		No comment
American Cancer Society		No comment

American Conservative Union Foundation   Never
This is the group that puts on CPAC, the annual mega-conference of
conservatives.

American Diabetes Association   Never

American Foundation for AIDS Research   Never

American Friends of Jordan River Village   No comment

American Friends of Magen David Adom   Never

American Friends of the Jaffa Institute   Never

American Heart Association   No comment

American Hotel and Lodging Education Foundation   No response

American Humane Association   Never

American Jewish Committee   2000 (amount not disclosed)

American Jewish Historical Society   Never

American ORT   No comment

American Red Cross   No comment

American Skin Association   No comment

American Society for the Prevention of Cruelty to Animals   No comment

American Spectator Foundation   Never

American Turkish Society   Never
Trump was "co-chair" of this group's 2012 gala. He gave $0.

American-Italian Cancer Foundation   Never

Americans for Prosperity Foundation   Never

Americares   No comment

Andrew Glover Youth Program   Never

Angels of Charity   No response

ANNIKA Foundation   No response

Anti-Defamation League   Never

Apollo Theater Foundation   Never

Arnold Palmer Medical Center Foundation   Never

⬚	Art for Life Foundation	Never
⬚	ASPCA	No comment
👥	Association to Benefit Children	Never
✱	Autism Project of Palm Beach County	No response
⬚	Autism Speaks	Never
👥	Bailey Baio Angel Foundation	No comment

Actor Scott Baio, the charity's founder, spoke at the Republican convention.

⬚	Bak Middle School of the Arts	Never
✱	Baseball Assistance Team	Never
👥	Beauvoir/Mississippi Sons of Confederate Veterans	No response
⬚	Best Buddies	Never
⬚	Bethesda-by-the-Sea Episcopal Church	No comment

This is the church where Trump got married to his wife, Melania, in Palm Beach, Fla.

⬚	Big Apple Association (Long Island)	Never
⬚	Big Apple Association (U.K.)	Never
⬚	Big Apple Circus	Never
⬚	Big Apple Greeter	Never
⬚	Big Dog Ranch Rescue	Never
⬚	Billy Graham Evangelistic Association	No comment
👥	Blanton Peale Institute	No response
👥	Border Patrol Foundation	Never
⬚	Boston Police Foundation	Never
⬚	Boy Scouts	No comment
⬚	Boynton Beach Community H.S.	Never
⬚	Boys and Girls Clubs of Broward County	No comment
👥	Boys and Girls Clubs of Palm Beach County	Never

One of Trump's golf courses in Florida is the site of a tournament benefitting this group on the day before the election.

▣	Boys and Girls Clubs of Stamford	Not since at least 2011
▣	Boys Club of New York	No comment
▣	Boys Town of Italy	No response
✱	Brain and Behavior Foundation (NARSAD Research Institute)	Never
✱	Brent Shapiro Foundation for Alcohol and Drug Awareness	Never
✱	Brewster Academy	No response
▣	Broadcasters Foundation of America	Never
▣	Broadway Cares	Never
▣	Bronx County Historical Society	Never
▣	Brooklyn Academy of Music	Never
▣	Brooklyn Bureau of Community Services	No response
▣	Brooklyn Hospital Center Foundation	Never
👥	Buckley School	No response
▣	Building with Books	No response
▣	Buoniconti Foundation/Miami Project	No comment
✱	Busey Foundation for Children's Kawasaki Disease	Never
▣	Calcutta Kids	Never
☰	Cancer Research Institute	Never
👥	Capuchin Food Pantry	Never
▣	Caring for Military Families/Elizabeth Dole Foundation	Never
✱	Caron Renaissance	No comment
✱	Carson Scholars Fund	No comment

In 2013, Trump was the "honorary chairman" of an event that benefited this charity, co-founded by retired neurosurgeon Ben Carson.

▣	CASA New Orleans	Never
▣	Catholic Charities of the Archdiocese of New York	No response
▣	Catholic Schools Foundation	No comment
✱	Cedars-Sinai, Sharon Osbourne Colon Cancer Program	Never

⊙	Celebrity Fight Night Foundation	Never
⊙	Center for Communication	Never
⊙	Central Iowa Shelter	Never
⊙	Central Park Conservancy	No comment
⊙	Chabad of East Boca Raton	Never
⊙	Chabad of Southampton	No comment
⊙	Chai Lifeline	Never
👥	Chapin School	No comment
👥	Charity:Water	No comment
⊙	Chicago Police Memorial Foundation	Never

In 2007, Trump told the IRS he'd given this group $5,000. In 2009, he told the IRS he'd taken it back. The Chicago charity says it never received a check in the first place.

⊙	Child Mind Institute	Never
⊙	Children's Aid Society	Never
⊙	Children's Hospital Foundation	No comment
⊙	Children's Medical Center, Omaha	Never
⊙	Children's Museum of Manhattan	Never
⊙	Children's Place at Home Safe	Never
⊙	Chris Evert Charities	Never
⊙	Citizens Against Government Waste	Never
⊙	Citizens United for Research in Epilepsy	Never

In 2012, Trump called in to MSNBC's "Morning Joe" to pledge $100,000 as part of a fundraiser led by David Axelrod, President Obama's longtime adviser. Axelrod had promised to shave his moustache if he could raise $1 million for the cause. Trump gave the money from his foundation, and gave $0 of his own.

⊙	Citizens United Foundation	No comment
👥	City College of NY	Never
⊙	City Parks Foundation	No comment

▣	Citymeals on Wheels	No comment
▣	Cleveland Clinic Florida	Never
✱	Coast Guard Foundation	Never
✱	College of Lake County (Ill.)	No comment

Trump donated an autograph for one of the college's fundraiser auctions.

▣	Columbia Grammar and Preparatory	No comment
≋	Columbia University Medical Center	No comment
▣	Columbus Citizens Foundation	No response
▣	Comic Relief	Never
▣	Community Foundation of West Chester-Liberty	Never

This is a hometown charity of former House speaker John A. Boehner (R-Ohio), a golfing buddy of Trump's. Boehner had mentioned the charity to Trump, and the mogul gave $5,000 from his foundation in 2013. He gave $0 of his own.

▣	Community Health Africa a Policy Solution	Never
▣	Comprehensive Autism Medical Assessment and Treatment Center of N.J.	Never
👥	Covenant Ballet Theater	Records unavailable
▣	Creedmoor Hospital	Never
▣	Crohn's and Colitis Foundation	No comment
≋	Crossroads Foundation (Cleveland)	Never
▣	Cystic Fibrosis Foundation	Never
▣	D.C. Preservation League	Never
▣	Damon Runyon Cancer Research Foundation	Never
▣	Dana-Farber Cancer Center	Never
✱	Darryl Strawberry Ministries	No response
▣	Disabled Veterans' Life Memorial (DAV)	Never
👥	Dominic Durden Memorial Scholarship	Never
✱	Donald J. Trump Foundation	2008 ($30,000)

Trump set up this charity in the late 1980s, and it originally served as a vehicle to give his own money away. In more recent years, the money in the charity has come primarily from others.

✱ Drumthwacket Foundation   Never
This charity maintains the historic New Jersey governor's mansion. Trump gave $40,000 from his foundation but nothing from himself. The Huffington Post reported that the foundation gifts came at a time when Trump was seeking state permission to build a private cemetery on a fairway at a course he owned in New Jersey.

⟦◎⟧ Dwyer High School Band (Palm Beach Gardens, Fla.)   Never

✱ Economic Club of Washington, D.C.   Never
Trump was invited to speak at an event in 2014 and paid for a table with $6,000 from his foundation. He has given $0 of his own.

⟦◎⟧ Elton John AIDS Foundation   Never

⟦◎⟧ enCourage Kids Foundation   Never

⟦◎⟧ Entertainment Industry Foundation/National
Colorectal Cancer Research Alliance   No response

👥 Eric Trump Foundation   Records Unavailable
This charity is run by one of Trump's sons. Eric Trump first told The Post that his father had given "hundreds of thousands" to his charity. Then, he said he couldn't recall one specific instance where his father gave anything.

⟦◎⟧ Eta Pi Chapter Foundation   No response

⟦◎⟧ Everglades Foundation   Never

⟦◎⟧ Exploring the Arts   No response

⟦◎⟧ Family Leader Foundation   No comment

⟦◎⟧ Fashion Footwear Charitable Foundation   Never

👥 FDNY Foundation   2008 ($5,000)

👥 Federal Drug Agents Foundation   Never

⟦◎⟧ Ferguson Library Foundation   Never

⟦◎⟧ First Presbyterian Church in Jamaica (Queens)   Not since at
                                                       least 2012

Trump's home church.

⟦◎⟧ Fisher House Never

In 2007, Trump settled a long-running dispute with the town of Palm Beach, Fla., over the height of a flagpole outside his Mar-a-Lago Club. The town agreed to waive $120,000 in unpaid fines, if Trump's club paid $100,000 to Fisher House, a charity that helps wounded service members. Trump instead used $100,000 from the Trump Foundation to pay that obligation, in a possible violation of laws against "self-dealing" by charity leaders.

[0] Florida Architecture Foundation — Never

[0] Florida Keys Reef Relief — Never

✱ Food for the Poor — Never
Trump was named the "national honorary chairman" of this charity's 2015 gala. Trump donated some Eric Trump-branded wine and made a brief appearance. He gave $0 in cash.

👥 Fordham University — No comment
Trump himself attended Fordham before studying business at the Wharton School at the University of Pennsylvania.

👥 Fore Life — Never

[0] Foundation for Long Island State Parks — No response

✱ Fresh Air Fund — 2008 (not disclosed)

✱ Friends of FDR and Donald J. Trump State Parks — Never
This volunteer group is dedicated to a New York state park, located on land that Trump donated after he struggled to get approvals for a golf course.

👥 Friends of Scotland — No response

✱ Friends of the Israel Defense Forces — 1997 (Not Disclosed)
This group provides welfare programs for Israeli military personnel. At a fundraiser in 2007, Trump promised to give $250,000 to the group. But he never paid. Another — unnamed — person paid in his stead.

[0] Friends of Veterans (Vermont) — Never

[0] Friends of Veterans (West Palm Beach) — Never

✱ Friends of Westchester County Parks — Never
In his most recent book, Trump notes that he got a "Green Space" award from this group. He was honored for a donation of land to the state of New York. He has never given any money to this group, from his foundation or from his own pocket.

🔲	Friendship Circle	No comment
🔲	Fund for Public Schools (NYC)	No response
✳	Gay Men's Health Crisis	Never
🔲	Generation Rescue	Never
👥	Georgetown University	Never
👥	Georgetown University Medical Center	Never
✳	German-American Hall of Fame	Never

Trump was inducted into this Hall of Fame in 2013, joining Dwight Eisenhower and Siegfried and Roy. The event was held at Trump Tower, so the Hall of Fame paid Trump more than $20,000 for the hall. Trump donated $1,000 from his foundation and nothing from his own pocket.

👥	GirlUp	Never

The Trump Organization's website lists this charity — which helps girls in developing countries — as a personal cause of Ivanka Trump, Trump's daughter. Donald Trump has never given any money to it, either from his foundation or from his own pocket.

🔲	Give A Smile to a Child	No response
🔲	Giving Back Fund	Never
🔲	Global Medical Relief Fund	Never
✳	GLSEN	Never
🔲	God's Love We Deliver	No comment
🔲	Golf Pros Beating Cancer	No comment
🔲	Graham Windham	No comment
👥	Grant Ronnebeck Foundation	No response
🔲	Green Beret Foundation	No response
👥	Greenwell Springs Baptist, La.	2016

Trump gave a $100,000 donation to this church, to aid flood-relief efforts.

🔲	Gucci Foundation	Not since at least 2008

Trump donated $107,500 from his foundation in 2008. Buzzfeed reported that this may have been to pay for a trip to Paris, which Trump bought at a charity auction.

⬛ Guggenheim Museum   No comment

✱ Guild Hall   No comment
In 2013, reports indicated that Trump bought a portrait of himself
and the artist promised to donate proceeds to Guild Hall. The artist
and the center declined to comment.

⬛ Gurwin Jewish Healthcare   Never

👥 Habitat for Humanity International   No comment
Trump bid $5,000 for a print of actor Rob Lowe's hands at a 2011
charity auction. But the charity wouldn't say if the money came from
Trump or his foundation.

✱ Hale House   Never
Trump's name is on a plaque outside the former site of this Harlem
charity, which cared for children who were born HIV-positive or
addicted to drugs. His gift was made in 1992 and was paid by one
of his Atlantic City casinos — which, at that point, was just out of
bankruptcy and half-owned by banks.

⬛ Harry Hurley in the Morning Golf Open   Never

⬛ Hawaii Children's Cancer Foundation   No comment

⬛ Health Care for the Homeless   Never
Trump gave $5,000 from the Trump Foundation to this group in
2010, as a wedding present for friends who were getting married —
and had asked for donations to this charity, in lieu of gifts.

👥 Heckscher Foundation/Take the Field   No response

⬛ Heroes to Heroes   Never

👥 Hill School   No comment

✱ Historical Society of Palm Beach County   Never
In his latest book, Trump says he was honored by this group — but
the award was for his work in restoring the Mar-a-Lago club, one of
Trump's money-making businesses. He has never given any money to
this group, from his foundation or from his own pocket.

✱ HollyRod Foundation   No response

👥 Hollywood Chamber of Commerce   Never

👥 Hollywood Historic Trust   Never

⬛ Homes for the Homeless   Never

👥	Hope for Children	No response
💿	Hope for Depression Research Foundation	No response
🗄	Hope House Ministries (Port Jefferson, N.Y.)	No comment
💿	Hospice of Palm Beach County	No comment
💿	Hospital for Special Surgery	No comment
✳	Hurricane Sandy N.J. Relief Fund	Never

At the Republican convention, New Jersey Gov. Chris Christie said that Trump had donated to a Sandy charity run by Christie's wife. But he didn't. Christie's spokesman said the governor "misspoke."

💿	Independence Fund	Never
💿	Indiana Golf Foundation	Never
💿	Indiana University	No comment
✳	Inner-City Foundation for Charity	2002
💿	Inner-City Scholarship Fund	Never
💿	Institute of Jewish Humanities	No response
✳	International Society of Palm Beach	Never
✳	Intrepid Fallen Heroes Fund	2005 (not disclosed)
✳	Intrepid Museum Foundation	2002
💿	Israel Cancer Research Fund	Never
✳	It Happened to Alexa Foundation	Never

Trump was the "honorary chairman" of a 2011 gala fundraiser for this charity, which helps victims of sexual assault. Although that title often carries an expectation of charitable donations, Trump gave nothing that year, from himself or his foundation

💿	Jaden's Ladder	Never
👥	Jamaica Hospital Medical Center	No comment

This medical center is the site of Trump Pavilion, a nursing home that was named after Trump's parents in the 1970s. Trump's foundation has never donated to it, but the medical center declined to say if Trump had ever given personally.

💿	James W. Foley Legacy Foundation	No response

A memorial foundation for a journalist killed by the Islamic State.

Trump spoke at a New Hampshire banquet where Foley was honored, then pledged a $25,000 donation.

⬚ Jersey City Museum — Never

⬚ Jewish Community Relations Council of NYC — No comment

⬚ Jewish Foundation for the Righteous — Not since at least 2000

✻ Jewish Guild Healthcare — Never

⬚ Jewish National Fund — No comment

⬚ Joe Torre Safe at Home Foundation — No comment

⬚ John A. Moran Eye Center — Never

⬚ Justice For All — Never

Trump's foundation erroneously listed a donation to this Kansas-based group on its tax filings. That mistake happened to mask another donation that violated IRS rules: a gift to And Justice for All, a similarly-named political group aligned with Florida Attorney General Pamela Bondi (R). At the time of that political gift, Bondi was considering whether to pursue an investigation of Trump University. The Trump Foundation blamed both mistakes—the illegal donation, and the tax filing that hid it from the IRS—on separate clerical errors.

⬚ Juvenile Diabetes Research Foundation — No comment

⬚ K9s for Warriors — Never

⬚ Kaleida Health Foundation — Never

✻ Kamp Kizzy — No comment

⬚ Kennedy Center for the Performing Arts — Never

✻ Kevin Guest House — Never

This is a gift by Dr. Donald L. "Skip" Trump, an oncologist, whose donations I found by accident while searching for Donald J. Trump's.

✻ KIND Fund, UNICEF — Never

Earlier this year, Trump sent a check from his foundation to MSNBC host Lawrence O'Donnell, made out to a charity that O'Donnell supports. The charity helps provide desks to schoolchildren in Malawi. O'Donnell said the check had been made out incorrectly, so he couldn't accept it. Trump never sent another check, made out the right way.

⬚ Kravis Center for the Performing Arts — Never

This arts center in West Palm Beach, Fla., has a seat named after Trump — the result of a 1989 donation from the Trump Foundation.

💬	Labyrinth Theater Company	Never
💬	Lance Armstrong (Livestrong) Foundation	Never
💬	LaSalle Academy	No comment
✳	Latino Commission on AIDS	Never
💬	Leaders in Furthering Education	No comment
💬	Lensic Foundation (Santa Fe, N.M.)	Never
💬	Leukemia and Lymphoma Society	No comment
👥	Liberty University	Never

Jerry Falwell Jr., Liberty's president, has been a vocal supporter of Trump during this campaign.

👥	Lifeheroic	Never
💬	Lincoln Center	Not since at least 2006
👥	Little Baby Face Foundation	Never
👥	Lone Survivor Foundation	Never

Marcus Luttrell, the former Navy SEAL who founded this veterans' charity, spoke at the Republican National Convention this year.

💬	Loudoun Arts Council	Never
👥	Louisana Flood Relief Fund	Never

Before Trump visited Louisiana to tour flooded areas, the state's governor suggested that Trump make a "sizable donation" to this fund, run by the Baton Rouge Area Foundation. Trump gave nothing, a spokeswoman said.

💬	Lubavitch Youth Organization	Never
👥	Madison Square Boys and Girls Club	No response
💬	Madison Square Park Conservancy	Never
💬	Maestro Cares	No response
✳	Magic Johnson Foundation	Never
✳	Make-A-Wish Foundation	Never
💬	Make-a-Wish of Southern Florida	No response

▣ Manhattan Ballet Company   Never

👥 Marble Collegiate Church   No comment

▣ March of Dimes   No comment

▣ Mariano Rivera Foundation   No response

✱ Marine Corps — Law Enforcement Foundation   2016 ($1 million)

In January, at a fundraiser for veterans' charities in Iowa, Trump said he had given $1 million from his own pocket. He did not actually give the money until four months later, when — under pressure from the media — Trump gave all $1 million to this charity, which helps the families of fallen Marines and federal officers. When asked if he had given the money because of media pressure, Trump called this reporter a "nasty guy."

▣ Marine Corps Scholarship Foundation   Never

▣ Martha Graham Center for Contemporary Dance   Never

✱ Martin B. Greenberg Foundation   Never

In 2012, Trump made a $158,000 donation from the foundation to this small charity. It appears to be the result of a legal dispute between Greenberg and one of Trump's golf courses, which began when Greenberg was denied a hole-in-one prize at a tournament. Greenberg said that Trump's staff had made the hole too short, which resulted in his hole-in-one being disqualified. This donation was made on the day that Trump's course and Greenberg informed the court they had settled their case.

▣ Massachusetts General Hospital   No comment

👥 Mayor's Fund to Advance New York City   Not since at least 2004

A city-run fund that helped New York City's recovery from Hurricane Sandy.

▣ McCarton Foundation   No response

👥 McConnell International Foundation   No response

▣ Memorial Sloan Kettering   No response

▣ Metropolitan Golf Association   No comment

▣ Metropolitan Museum of Art   No comment

▣ Metropolitan Opera   No comment

⬤	Michael J. Fox Foundation	Never
⬤	Mill River Collaborative	Never
⬤	Montefiore Foundation	Never
⬤	MorseLife Foundation	No response
👥	Mourning Family Foundation	No comment
⬤	Mt. Sinai Children's Center Foundation	No comment
⬤	Muscular Dystrophy Association	No comment
✱	Museum of Jewish Heritage	2003
⬤	Museum of the City of New York	Never
🗌	N.Y. Blood Center	No comment
⬤	N.Y. Historical Society	Never
⬤	N.Y. Junior Tennis	Never
✱	N.Y. Landmarks Conservancy	1992 ($1,000)
👥	N.Y. Military Academy	No comment

Donald Trump attended high school here. He has donated more than $30,000 from his Donald J. Trump Foundation. The school declined to comment about any personal gifts.

⬤	N.Y. Police & Fire Widows' and Children's Benefit Fund	No comment

During the Republican National Convention, former New York mayor Rudy Giuliani said that Trump had given donations to the families of fallen police and firefighters. This is New York's main charity to benefit those families.

⬤	N.Y. Rescue Workers Detox Project	No response
⬤	N.Y. Shakespeare Festival	1995 ($2,000)
✱	N.Y. State Adopt-A-Highway	No response

An "adopt-a-highway" sign on part of the Henry Hudson Parkway has Trump's name on it. The city of New York said the Trump Organization, Trump's business, paid the fee. It did not say how much was paid.

✱	N.Y. Vietnam Vets Memorial Fund	1995 ($200,000)

Trump made two large donations to veterans' causes in New York: In 1985, he gave $1 million to help build a Vietnam veterans memorial in the city, and in 1995 he gave an amount estimated between $200,000 and $400,000 to help finance a parade honoring veterans on the 50th anniversary of the end of World War II.

[0]	NAACP Legal Defense Fund	No response
[0]	NAACP New York City	No response
[0]	NAACP New York State Conference	No response
[0]	NASCAR Foundation	No comment
[0]	Nat Moore Foundation	Never
✸	Natalie Gulbis Boys and Girls Club	Never

Pro golfer Natalie Gulbis, a speaker at the Republican National Convention, thanked Trump for his help in starting this Boys and Girls Club clubhouse in Nevada. Trump has not donated, either from his foundation or from his own pocket.

[0]	National Children's Oral Health Foundation (America's Tooth Fairy)	Never
[0]	National Football Foundation	Never
✸	National Inclusion Project	Never
[0]	National Italian American Foundation	Never
[0]	National Jewish Health	Never
[0]	National Multiple Sclerosis Society	Never
[0]	National Museum of Catholic Art and History	Records unavailable
✸	National Network to End Domestic Violence	Never
✸	National Society of Arts and Letters	Never

Trump was honorary chairman of this group's East Coast Florida chapter's Red Rose Gala in 2015. He gave $0, from his foundation or from his own pocket.

[0]	National Wildlife Federation	Never
[0]	Natural High	No response
✸	NephCure	No comment
[0]	New Destiny Christian Center	No response

🔘	New York Center for Living	Never
🔘	New York Jets Foundation	Never
🔘	New York Legal Assistance Group	Never
🔘	New York Marine Corps Council	Records unavailable
🔘	New York Pops	Never
🔘	New York Presbyterian Hospital	No comment
🔘	New York Restoration Project	Never
🔘	New York Times Neediest Cases	Never
🔘	New Yorkers for Parks	Never
🔘	Newark Museum Association	Never
🔘	NFL Player Care Foundation	Never
🗄	Niagara University	2000 (not disclosed)
🔘	Nicklaus Children's Health Care Foundation	Never
✳	North Shore Animal League America	No comment
👥	North York Harvest Food Bank	No response
🔘	NYC Parks and Recreation	Never
🔘	NYC Police Foundation	No comment
👥	NYU Hospital for Joint Diseases	No response
👥	Operation 300	No comment

A charity to honor fallen Navy SEAL Aaron Woods, whose mother has spoken out on Trump's behalf.

👥	Operation Backpack	No comment
🔘	Operation Smile	No comment
✳	Opportunity Village	Never
🔘	Orthopaedic Foundation	Never
👥	Pace University	No response
🔘	Painted Turtle Gang Camp Foundation	Never
🔘	Paley Center for Media	No comment

◉ Paley Foundation   No comment

✱ Palm Beach Habilitation Center   Never

✱ Palm Beach Opera   Never
Trump was named the "international honorary chairman" for this
group's gala in 2009. He gave $0 that year, from his foundation or
from himself.

◉ Palm Beach Police Foundation   Never

◉ Palm Beach Preservation Foundation   No comment

✱ Palm Beach Symphony   Never

◉ Palm Beach Zoo   Never

◉ Palmetto Family Council   Never

◉ Pancreatic Cancer Action Network   Never

◉ Partners for Patriots   Never

◉ Partnership for the Homeless   Records unavailable

✱ Physicians Committee for Responsible Medicine   No comment

◉ Pin Down Bladder Cancer   No response

✱ Planned Parenthood   No comment
Trump has praised some of Planned Parenthood's work, while also
threatening to cut off its federal funding if it continues to perform
abortions.

✱ Play for P.I.N.K. (Breast Cancer Research Foundation)   Never

✱ Police Athletic League of Buffalo   2004 ($5,000)

✱ Police Athletic League of New York   2009 ($5,000-$9,999)
This is the only organization that reported receiving a personal
donation from Trump between 2008 — the last time he gave to his
own Donald J. Trump Foundation — and this May. It may also be a
bookkeeping error, with the PAL counting a donation from Trump's
foundation as a gift from the man himself. That happened in other
years' data, but the PAL says it cannot tell if it happened this year.

◉ Princess Grace Foundation   Never

👥 Professional Women in Construction   No response

◉ Project Veritas   Never

✱	Promises 2 Kids	Never
⬤	Prostate Cancer Foundation	Never
✱	Protect Our Winters	Never
⬤	Puppy Jake	Never
⬤	Queens Library Foundation	2004 ($1,000)
👥	Rainbow/PUSH Coalition	No response
⬤	Ramp Church	Never

In 2012, when Trump visited Liberty University, a student handed Trump a letter asking for a $1,000 donation to her Virginia church. He gave the money from the foundation.

⬤	Reporters Committee for Freedom of the Press	Never
✱	Right to Play	Never
🝫	Riverdale Country School	No comment
⬤	Robin Hood Foundation	No comment
⬤	Ronald McDonald House of N.Y.	Never
⬤	Ronald Reagan Presidential Library	Never
⬤	Rose Brucia Foundation	Never
✱	Roswell Park Alliance/Roswell Park Cancer Institute	Never

This was a personal donation to charity — but from the wrong Donald Trump. Dr. Donald L. "Skip" Trump, an oncologist who previously ran this Buffalo cancer center, has given generously to a variety of causes. Donald J. Trump, the presidential candidate, did once give to the cancer center from his foundation, after the other Donald Trump asked him.

⬤	Rubin Museum of Art	Never
⬤	Rush Philanthropic Arts Foundation	Never
⬤	Salvation Army	No comment
⬤	Samaritan's Purse	No comment
⬤	Samuel Waxman Cancer Research Foundation	Never
👥	School of American Ballet	Never

Ivanka Trump, Trump's daughter, studied ballet here as a young

woman. Trump gave $16,750 from his foundation in the late 1980s
and early 1990s, but nothing from his own pocket.

👥	Second Harvest Food Bank, N.C.	No response
🔟	Seeds of Peace	Never
🔟	Seton Hall Law School	No response
👥	Sgt. Brandon Mendoza Memorial Foundation	Never
🔟	Shaare Zedek Medical Center	Never
🔟	Shaun O'Hara Foundation	No response
👥	Shayley Estes Memorial Scholarship Fund	Never
🔟	Shine Global	Never
🔟	Shore Memorial Health Foundation	No response
🔟	Simon Wiesenthal Center	Never
🔟	Skyscraper Museum	Never
🔟	Small World Big Life	Never
👥	Smile Train	No comment

Donald Trump Jr. is on this organization's board. The Donald J. Trump
Foundation does not appear to have donated to it, but the organization declined comment about any gifts from Trump personally.

🔟	Somer Sunshine Foundation	No response
🔟	Special Operations Warrior Foundation	No comment
🔟	St. Francis Food Pantries	No comment
✱	St. John the Divine	2002 (not disclosed)
🔟	St. Jude Children's Research Hospital	No comment
🔟	St. Luke's Community Services	Never
🔟	Stamford Center for the Arts	No comment
🔟	Stamford Museum and Nature Center	Never
👥	Stand Up To Cancer	No comment

Actor Rob Lowe, an acquaintance of Trump's, has raised money for
this cause.

| ✱ | Starkey Hearing Foundation | No response |

Starlight Children's Foundation — Never

Statue of Liberty — Ellis Island Foundation — Never

Sunrise Day Camp — Never

Susan G. Komen Foundation — Never

In 2012, Trump purchased a football helmet signed by then-Denver Broncos quarterback Tim Tebow — as well as a Tebow jersey — for $12,000 at an auction run by this breast-cancer charity. He paid with money from the foundation, despite IRS rules that say a nonprofit's leaders cannot use money meant for charity to buy goods for themselves.

Tanzanian Children's Fund — Never

Temple Shaare Zion — No comment

The Able Trust — No response

The Church, St. Amant, La. — No response

CNN reported that Trump had donated a truckload of "stuff" at this church in an area of Louisiana hard-hit by flooding

The Foundation for Jamiel Shaw II — No response

The Hawn Foundation — Never

The Remembrance Project — Never

Theater Development Fund — Never

Tiger Woods Foundation — No comment

Turn 2 Foundation — No response

Twin Towers Fund — Never

During the Republican National Convention, former New York mayor Rudy Giuliani said that Trump had given donations to the families of fallen police and firefighters. This was a charity set up to help those families after the Sept. 11 terrorist attacks.

Tyrone S. Woods Wrestling Foundation — Never

A foundation honoring a former Navy SEAL slain in the attacks on U.S. diplomatic compounds in Benghazi, Libya. Woods's father has endorsed Trump for president.

UCLA Foundation — Never

UJA-Federation — No comment

✱ Unicorn Children's Foundation   Never

This charity gave Trump two honors at the same charity gala in 2008, naming him "grand honorary chairman" and giving him the "Shining Star Award." Although such honors often come with an expectation of a large donation, Trump gave $5,000 from his foundation and $0 from his own pocket.

✱ United Cerebral Palsy   2001 (not disclosed)

✱ United Hatzalah   No comment

In 2014, according to media reports, Trump publicly promised to give $100,000 to this charity, which funds emergency medical services in Israel. The available records from his foundation show no such gifts. The charity would not comment as to whether Trump had fulfilled the pledge.

◉ United Negro College Fund   No comment

◉ United Way of NYC   No comment

✱ University of California at Berkeley Journalism School   Never

◉ University of Illinois Foundation   No comment

✱ University of Pennsylvania Press   No comment

◉ USTA   Never

◉ V Foundation   No comment

In 2013, Trump wanted the V Foundation to hold a fundraiser at his winery in Virginia. Trump's foundation gave them $10,000 that summer. He got the fundraiser.

◉ Veterans of Foreign Wars   Never

Trump's foundation gave repeated, very small donations to the VFW in the 1980s and 1990s but hasn't given since a $100 check in 1999. He has never given his own money. The VFW says that two other people named Donald Trump, in Indiana and Pennsylvania, have given more.

✱ Villagers Theatre   Not since at least 1998

This community theater in central New Jersey has a seat marked with a plaque that lists Trump's name and the name of a casino he owned in New Jersey. The theater's leaders say they don't know what Trump did to get his name on the plaque, or if he even visited. Whatever he gave, it was at least 18 years ago.

◉ Waterfront Alliance   Never

💵	Waterfront Center (D.C.)	Never
💵	Waterfront Center (N.Y.)	Never
💵	Wayuu Taya Foundation	No response
✻	West Side Montessori School	Never
👥	Westchester Golf Association Caddie Scholarship Fund	No comment
💵	Westport Country Playhouse	2003
👥	Wharton Club of NYC	No response
👥	Wharton/UPenn	No comment

Trump graduated from the Wharton School at the University of Pennsylvania.

💵	White Plains Hospital Center	Never
💵	William J. Clinton Foundation	Never

Trump's foundation gave $110,000 total in 2009 and 2010 to this foundation run by former president Bill Clinton and Trump's current Democratic opponent, Hillary Clinton. He never gave money of his own.

💵	Wolfsonian-FIU	No comment
💵	Women In Need	Never
✻	Wounded Warrior Project	Never

In 2013, Trump praised this charity, chosen by Celebrity Apprentice contestant Trace Adkins. "Donate to an Injured Warrior today," Trump wrote on Twitter.

 DAVID A. FAHRENTHOLD is a political reporter for the Washington Post's national staff. He has worked for the Post since 2000, when he arrived as a summer intern on the city desk. Since then, Fahrenthold has covered the D.C. police, the environment, New England, Congress, federal bureaucracy, and presidential and Congressional elections. During the 2016 election, Fahrenthold wrote extensively about Donald Trump's unfulfilled promises to donate to charity – and about the Donald J. Trump Foundation, a charity run by the then-candidate that appeared to violate federal rules by using its money to buy large portraits of Trump, and to pay off the legal settlements of Trump's businesses. He also revealed the existence of a 2005 video, taken during a taping of "Access Hollywood," in which Trump made extremely lewd comments about groping women.

For his 2016 campaign reporting, Fahrenthold was awarded the Pulitzer Prize for national reporting. He was also honored with a George Polk Award for Political Reporting from Long Island University and the Toner Prize for Excellence in Political Reporting. He is a native of Houston, Texas, and a 2000 graduate of Harvard University. He now lives in Washington with his wife, Elizabeth Lewis, and his daughters Alexandra, 4, and Stella, age 1.

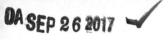
CPSIA information can be obtained
at www.ICGtesting.com
Printed in the USA
BVOW06s1352200417
R7915900001B/R79159PG481769BVX2B/2/P